Police and the Mentally Ill

A Field Guide for Police Professionals

By

Robert D. Newell, M.A. Psychology

Chief of Police (Retired)

D1563990

The Cover

Parkersburg, WV, police officers R.D. Newell, Steve Plum, and Doug McLain removing a mentally ill man from on top of an alter at a local church after he began eating pages from a bible and climbed to the top.

About the Author

Robert D. Newell began his law enforcement career in 1972 with the City of Parkersburg, West Virginia, Police Department, retiring in 1993. He returned to his department after being appointed as Chief of Police and served from 2002 until 2006.

As Chief of Police, the author initiated and lead the department through the process of becoming the first police department in West Virginia to obtain accreditation through the Commission on the Accreditation of Law Enforcement Agencies (CALEA), and remains one of just a few departments in the state with the accreditation.

Before being appointed Chief of Police, Mr. Newell served as a Magistrate Court judge for two years before accepting a position of Associate Professor of the Criminal Justice Program at Washington State Community College in Marietta, Ohio.

The author was an adjunct faculty member for over 20 years at West Virginia

University at Parkersburg where he taught multiple criminal justice courses and the behavioral sciences. Mr. Newell developed the first Forensic Psychology course at WVU-Parkersburg and taught the course for several years.

Mr. Newell is a certified Law Enforcement Instructor and has taught dozens of police officers in seminars on Managing the Mentally Ill as well as other in-service and supervisory level subjects. He previously served on the Law Enforcement Professional Standards Subcommittee of the Governor's Commission on Crime, Delinquency, and Corrections.

Mr. Newell received his Master of Arts Degree in Psychology from Marshall University Graduate College after obtaining a Regents Bachelor of Arts from Fairmont State College.

Table of Contents

I.   Preface
14

II.   How to Use this Manual
18

III.   Understanding Mental Illness and Misperceptions to Avoid
22

IV.   Judging and Recognizing Abnormal Behavior
26

V.   Scene Management and Intervention Techniques
30

VI.   Mental Disorders Commonly Encountered by Police
38

Alcohol Induced Disorders
38

Alzheimer's Disease (Dementia)
40

Amnesia (Dissociative Amnesia)
42

Antisocial   Personality   Disorder
(Sociopath / Psychopath)
43

Autism Spectrum Disorders
45

Bipolar Disorder
47

Brief Psychotic Disorder
50

Cannabis Intoxication
52

Cannabis Withdrawal
53

Conduct Disorder
54

Delirium
56

Delusional Disorders
58

Depressive   Disorder   (Major
Depression)   60

Dissociative Identity Disorder
(Multiple Personalities)
62
Excited Delirium
63
Hallucinations
65
Hallucinogen Intoxication
66
Hallucinogen Persisting Perception
Disorder (Flashbacks)
67
Intellectual Disabilities
69
Intermittent Explosive Disorder
72
Kleptomania
73
Opioid Intoxication
74
Oppositional Defiant Disorder
75
Panic Attacks
77

Paraphilias (Abnormal Sexual Behavior)
78

Phencyclidine (PCP) Intoxication
80

Posttraumatic Stress Disorder-PTSD
82

Pyromania
84

Schizophrenia Spectrum Disorders
85

Substance Induced Disorders
87

Suicide Behavior
90

Suicide by Cop
95

Managing Mental Illness among police officers
98

VII.   Involuntary Emergency Commitment Laws in Each State.
100

VIII.   Use of Force in Civil Commitments & Non-Criminal Behavior - U.S. Court of Appeals for the Fourth Circuit Opinion
118

IX.   Case Studies   122

Use of Force- Armstrong v. Town of Pinehurst.
122

Use of Force – Failure to Train – Quintonio Leggier and Chicago Police
124

Duty to Warn - Tarasoff v. the Regents of   the University of California Medical Center.
126

Schizophrenia – Iman Morales and New York Police Dept.
128

Schizoaffective Disorder – James Boyd and Albuquerque, NM Police
130

Schizophrenia – Deborah Danner and New York Police Dept.
132

Antisocial Personality (Sociopath) Jeffrey Dahmer, Milwaukee Police.
134

Developmental & Intellectual Disorder – Robert Ethan Saylor Frederick Maryland Sheriff Office.
136

Command Hallucinations – Esteban Santiago, Ft. Lauderdale Airport Shooting.
138

Schizophrenia – Charleena Lyles Seattle Police.
140

Bipolar Disorder – Rubin Herrera Los Angeles Police.
142

Delusional Disorder – Margaret Mary "Peggy" Ray Stalking Case.
143

Oppositional Defiant Disorder – School Resource Officer Ben Fields

Richland County Sheriff's Office.
145

PTSD – Suicide by Cop – Nikkolas Lookabill.
 146

Intermittent Explosive Disorder – Eric Smith Bath New York.
148

Substance Induced Disorder – Alton Sterling, Baton Rouge.
149

Suicide by Cop – Micah Jester and Austin, Texas Police.
150

Autism – Eric Parsa Jefferson County, LA
152

Autism – Linden Cameron – Salt Lake PD
153

PTSD – Nitro, WV Police Department
154

Suicidal Behavior – Dustin Pigeon
155

Excited Delirium – Adam Trammell West Milwaukee
156

Excited Delirium – Elijah McClain Aurora, Colorado
158

Excited Delirium - Daniel Prude – Rochester, NY
159

X.   Report Writing – Terms and phrases to avoid involving incidents.
162

APPENDIX 165

a. Medications Commonly Associated with Mental Disorders

b. Comprehensive Alphabetical list of both Generic and Brand name psychotropic medications.
112.0

c. Definitions of Associated terms. References

Preface

Police as Mental Health First Responders

Police officers have become the first responders in mental health crisis situations. Mental illness is the only illness whereas when a crisis is occurring, the police are called to intervene in most cases.

Each year, approximately two million mentally ill persons are incarcerated in state and local jails according to the National Association of Mental Illness, which is ten times the number who are committed to state funded mental health facilities. The three largest mental health providers in the United States are consistently the Cook County Jail in Chicago, the Los Angeles County Jail, and Ryker's Island in New York. (NAMI)

According to the Treatment Advocacy Center and others, about a fourth of fatal shootings by police are mentally ill persons. In 2015, there were 243 mentally ill subjects killed by police. Seventy-five (75) were suicidal. Out of the 243, around two thirds

(168) happened as a result of calls to police from family members, many who had called police on previous occasions.

The lack of training results in tragic deaths and lawsuits each year. These are outcomes that could be prevented with proper training.

Calls for service come from a variety of complaints and officers are often unaware the call involves a mentally ill person until they arrive. The nature of calls includes suspicious or disorderly persons, assaults and domestic violence, stalking, suicide attempts, homicide, infanticide, and other criminal activity.

According to the National Alliance on Mental Illness (NAMI), approximately 61.5 million Americans experience a mental illness in a given year and about 13.6 million Americans live with a serious mental illness. A majority never receive mental health services.

Within the homeless population, which law enforcement officers deal with on a daily basis, 46% live with a serious mental illness and/or substance addiction.

This guide is designed to help police officers in the field to better understand and better manage these calls for service involving the mentally ill.

How to Use This Manual

This manual is intended to help officers to determine whether or not the person's behavior is abnormal, help gauge the level or seriousness of the behavior, and provide information on how to approach or manage the presenting characteristics on the scene of a call for service involving someone suffering from mentally illness.

The manual is not intended to be used by police officers to try to diagnose the specific mental disorder they are dealing with on a call. This manual is also not intended to replace comprehensive training for police officers.

Section IV. A quick reference guide to understanding mental illness and dismissing any preconceived notions and misconceptions by police officers about mentally illness.

Section V. An outline of behaviors that should be considered as abnormal.

Section VI. Suggestions useful in all cases in approaching someone who is mentally ill. While all of them do not apply to every situation, some apply to all mental health crisis situations.

Section VII. Brief and edited mental disorders which police officers commonly face in the field on calls for their service. Included with each disorder is a list of characteristics that may be readily apparent to the officer.

Under each mental disorder are scene management techniques taken from the main list that may be pertinent to a specific disorder that is recognizable. For instance, approaching someone who is autistic requires action or inaction that is different from other disorders.

Section VIII. Condensed and edited Emergency Involuntary Commitment Laws for each state.

Section IX. A breakdown of the latest court rulings on the use of force in civil or mental commitments and non-criminal behavior by mentally ill persons.

Section X. A summary of recent cases involving interaction between police officers and mentally ill persons that have resulted in the deaths or lawsuits. They are not intended to assign fault to the officers or the mentally ill person, but serve as an example of things to consider and protect officers when answering these calls for service.

Section XI. A guide to medications that are commonly associated with certain mental illnesses that may be present or found during these calls for service.

Section XII. A glossary of common terms associated with mental illness and related definitions.

Section XIII. A comprehensive alphabetical list of both generic and brand name psychotropic medications.

Section XIV. References

Understanding Mental Illness

Common Misconceptions

- All people who are mentally ill are violent, dangerous, or homicidal.

  Fact - Mental Illness alone does not cause violence. Mentally ill persons are more likely to harm themselves of be victims of violence.

- Those who are mentally ill will always be ill and their condition will never vary.

  Fact – Some may never overcome their illness, but most are quite able to function normally through treatment and medications.

- All mentally ill people are insane and incompetent.

22

Fact - Insanity and incompetency are legal terms, not medical terms.
Insanity is the inability to distinguish right from wrong in a criminal act due to a mental disorder.

Fact - Incompetency is the inability to understand proceedings and help with their own defense.

- The behavior and feelings of the mentally ill are completely different from the mentally healthy.

Fact – In many cases their feelings may be more profound but not necessarily different. For example, many people have feelings of anxiousness, sadness, or even paranoia about certain things but are able to manage them without intervention.

- You can't believe anything a mentally ill person tells you.

Fact - Absent delusions or hallucinations, those with mental illness are quite capable of understanding and telling the truth.

Judging and Recognizing Abnormal Behavior

Common Indicators to Consider

- Is the person's behavior appropriate for the time, place and circumstances?

- Can they answer simple mental status questions regarding orientation and memory?
    - What is your name?
    - What day and time is it now?
    - Where are you now?
    - Who is the president?
    - Who was the president before them?
    - Name three famous presidents.

- Does the person have a significant loss of memory of important personal information?

- Does the person report hearing voices, smelling odors, or seeing visions?

- Does the person talk to themselves?

- Does the person exhibit grandiosity, that is, do they believe they are someone of importance like a president or God, etc.?

- Does the person relate feelings of persecution, for example, they believe without evidence someone is trying to poison them?

- Does the person relate characteristics of paranoia, for example, do they believe without evidence they are being followed by the CIA or FBI, or ISIS?

- Does the person appear overly frightened or easily startled?

- Does the person appear depressed?

- Does the person relate unrealistic physical complaints, such as being infested with fleas or ailments contrary to any medical evidence?

- Has the persons behavior changed drastically over a short period of time?

- Does the person relate command hallucinations which are voices commanding them to act?

Note: See the Case Study of Esteban Santiago Fort Lauderdale Airport Shootings.

Scene Management Techniques

- Involve more than one officer, preferably in a uniform if possible.
    - Aggression and violence *may* be reduced if you are readily recognizable as a police officer.
    - The amount of force necessary may be reduced.

- Notify and involve mental health professionals if practical and available.

- Never leave the person unattended or alone.
    - Officers have a right to ensure their own safety.
    - Some mentally ill persons can be unpredictable.

- Help regain control of the scene.
    - Do not agitate the person further.

- Do not crowd the person. Give them body space.
- Do not start out expecting a confrontation or respond to hostility with hostility.
- Avoid quick movements that may be interpreted as aggressive.
- Do not bait or challenge the person into action or confrontation.
- Do not squabble with family members present, for example, telling them that "this is a police matter now", etc.
- Ask unnecessary people to leave the room.
- Comply with reasonable request, such as, "don't shine your flashlight on me" or "may I smoke a cigarette"?

- Give the person assurances that they won't be harmed.

- o Remain calm, professional, and give reassurance.
- o Involve family members if the circumstances warrant.

- Communication skills are key to a successful resolution.
  - o Be respectful and avoid unnecessary touching.
  - o Use simple sentences and speak calmly and clearly.
  - o Do not shout orders or use intimidation tactics.
  - o Do not threaten or use sarcasm.
  - o Do not criticize or lecture the person.
  - o Avoid patronizing or authoritative statements.

- Be Patient.
  - o Mental illnesses are biological brain diseases that you can't talk someone out of just like you can't talk someone out of having kidney or liver diseases.

- Make sure the person is not physically ill.
    - There are a variety of toxins, medicines, and medical conditions that can mimic mental illnesses.
    - Bring any behavioral problem to the attention of trained medical personnel as soon as practical, if necessary.

- Do not agree or disagree with delusions.
    - Delusions do not go away with reasoning.
    - Try to change the conversation back to reality.

- Beware of a sudden return to reality.
    - Mental illness can be unpredictable and moods may shift abruptly.

- o Do not form a sense of security just because no laws have been broken.

- Do not lie or try to deceive the person.
  - o Absent delusions or hallucinations, mental ill persons are quite capable of understanding and telling the truth.
  - o Any hope of gaining cooperation or their confidence will be lost.

- Do not rely on the presentation of weapons to control the scene unless the subject is armed or lives are in danger.
  - o The presentation of weapons may unnecessarily aggravate the situation.

- Take all threats of suicide seriously.
  - o Most people who commit suicide have threatened or

communicated their intentions previously.

- o Threats of suicide may not be for the purpose of wanting attention as many believe.

- Take all threats made toward others seriously.
  - o There are no confidentiality privileges for a mentally ill person who makes a credible threat of harm against someone.
  - o There is a duty to warn a third party if a credible threat has been made unknowingly toward them in many states.
  - o There may also be a duty to provide adequate protection to a third party who has been threatened with harm.

Note: See Case Study of Tarasoff v. the Regents of the University of California Medical Center

<u>Note:</u> The duty to warn or duty to protect laws and rulings differ from state to state. However, it has been widely recognized that colleges and universities, including campus police officers, may be liable for failing to warn a third party of threats against them.

Mental Disorders Commonly Encountered by Police Officers (Alphabetically)

Alcohol Induced Disorders

In addition to intoxication or withdrawal, the heavy and prolonged use of alcohol can result in Delirium, Dementia, Amnesia, and Psychosis.

- Characteristics which may be readily apparent to police officers:

    o Recent use of alcohol.
    o Lack of memory or failure to recall personal information.
    o Inability to recognize people or objects.
    o Inability to focus, maintain attention, or concentrate.
    o Language and communications deficits.
    o Disorientation and perceptual distortions.
    o Hallucinations
    o Delusions

- Scene Management Techniques:

    o Involve more than one officer if possible.
    o Do not leave the person alone or unattended.
    o Make sure the person is not physically ill.
    o Involve medical personnel if necessary.
    o Do not agitate the person further
    o Avoid quick aggressive or hostile movements.
    o Do not shout orders or use intimidation.
    o Do not agree or disagree with delusions.

Some States and jurisdictions allow detention for <u>Emergency Evaluation</u> persons who present a danger to themselves or others due to <u>Substance Dependence</u> or addiction.

Alzheimer's Disease (Dementia)

Alzheimer's is the most common Neurocognitive Disorder previously referred to as one type of Dementia.

- Characteristics which may be readily apparent to police officers:
    - Noticeable deficits in memory, such as name, address, or other personal information.
    - Failure to recognize objects and people.
    - Depressed mood.
    - Reduced attention and awareness capabilities.
    - Delusions of jealousy, paranoia, persecution. *
    - Irritability, agitation, combativeness, and wandering away. *
    - Deficits in language and communications skills.

*Substantial threats or attempts to harm others may be cause for involuntary commitments.

- Scene Management Techniques:

  - Give the person reassurance they will not be harmed.
  - Involve another officer or family member.
  - Involve mental health professionals if available.
  - Never the leave the person unattended or alone.
  - Use simple sentences and speak calmly and clearly.
  - Do not agree with or argue with their delusional beliefs, if any.
  - Avoid unnecessary touching and do not crowd the person.
  - Do not shout orders, threaten, or use intimidation.
  - Avoid quick movements that may be interpreted as aggressive.
  - Be patient.

Some States and jurisdictions allow detention for <u>Emergency Evaluation</u> when a person is <u>Gravely Disabled</u> and unable to

satisfy the need for basic care, such as food, shelter, and medical care.

Amnesia (Dissociative Amnesia Disorder)

Dissociative Amnesia involves the loss of memory of selected periods of time or of selected events, usually as a result of a traumatic event. A complete loss of memory of one's personal history is rare.

- Characteristics which may be readily apparent to police officers:
    - An inability to recall important personal information such as their name, address, and personal history.
    - The inability is not attributed to apparent intoxication by alcohol or drugs.

- Scene Management Techniques:
    - There are a variety of toxins and medications that mimic mental illnesses. Bring any issues

involving amnesia to the attention of medical personnel as soon as practical.

- o Bring any issues involving amnesia to the attention of mental health professionals as soon as practical.
- o Be patient as memory may not return in a short amount of time.
- o Involve family members if available and necessary.
- o Don't argue with the person's beliefs of their identity.

Some States and jurisdictions allow detention for <u>Emergency Evaluation</u> when a person is <u>Gravely Disabled</u> and unable to satisfy the need for basic care, such as food, shelter, and medical care.

Antisocial Personality Disorder (Sociopath / Psychopath)

Antisocial Personality Disorder is often associated with Criminal Behavior. APD was previously referred to as Sociopathic and

Psychopathic Disorders. Unfortunately, their characteristics are not readily exhibited or apparent which can be a danger to officers.

- Characteristics of Antisocial Personality Disorder:
    - o Repeated failures to obey the laws, rules, and rights of others.
    - o Deceitfulness
    - o Absence of guilt or remorse
    - o Absence of anxiety even when confronted by police
    - o Impulsive acts without consideration of consequences
    - o Irresponsibility in meeting obligations, financial or otherwise.
    - o Irritability and aggressive behavior.
    - o Failure to learn from previous mistakes, repeat offending of laws.
    - o Charismatic and manipulative behavior.

Note: See Case Study of Jeffrey Dahmer and Milwaukee Police Officers

Autism Spectrum Disorder

Autism is a Neurodevelopment Disorder usually identified in the first 2 years of a child's development and involves delayed or restricted communications skills, social skills, and motor skills.

- o Characteristics which may be readily apparent to police officers:
  - o The inability to communicate properly, lack of normal engaging conversations, lack of eye contact with officers or others, and lack of non-verbal communications skills.
  - o They may be completely non-verbal.
  - o The exhibition of repetitive or ritualistic patterns of behavior and/or verbal behavior.

- o Extreme distress at changes in routines.
- o Extreme distress at environmental changes such as lights, sounds, or touching.

- o Scene Management Techniques:
  - o Avoid unnecessary touching.
  - o Use simple sentences and speak calmly and clearly.
  - o Involve family members if available.
  - o Avoid authoritative or intimidating statements.
  - o Comply with reasonable requests, e.g., "please don't shine the flashlight on me."
  - o Do not squabble with family members who are present.
  - o Ask unnecessary visitors to leave the room.
  - o Don't crowd the person.
  - o Bring to the attention of mental health professionals, if necessary, as soon as practical.

Some States and jurisdictions allow detention for <u>Emergency Evaluation</u> when a person is <u>Gravely Disabled</u> and unable to satisfy the need for basic care, such as food, shelter, and medical care.

Bipolar Disorders

Bipolar Disorder was formerly referred to as Manic-Depressive Disorder. The disorder involves both depressed moods and manic episodes.
- o Characteristics which may be readily apparent to police officers:
  - o Manic Episodes:
    - o Inflated self-esteem and grandiose beliefs of themselves.
    - o Overly talkative with a pressure or urge to keep talking.
    - o Racing thoughts and ideas are presented.
    - o Agitation.

- Attention is easily distracted.
- Impulsive self-damaging acts without consideration of the consequences. *

- Major Episodes of Depression:
  - Depressed and sad mood, feelings of worthlessness.
  - Fatigue and loss of energy.
  - Agitation.
  - Inability to concentrate or make decisions.
  - Thoughts of death or suicide.
  - Plans and/or attempts at suicide. *

- Scene Management Techniques:
  - Take all threats of suicide seriously. *
  - Be patient and professional.
  - Don't start out expecting a confrontation.

48

- o Help regain control of the scene when necessary.
- o Involve more than one officer when possible.
- o Do not shout orders, threaten, or use sarcasm.
- o Avoid unnecessary quick or aggressive movements.
- o Do not rely on your weapon to control the situation unless they are armed.
- o Comply with reasonable requests, such as, "please don't shine your flashlight at me."

*Substantial threats or attempts to harm themselves or others may be cause for involuntary commitments.

Note: See the Case Study of Rubin Herrera and LAPD

Brief Psychotic Disorder

A Brief Psychotic Disorder is a brief and sudden occurrence of a behavioral disturbance involving at least one characteristic of delusions, hallucinations, or incoherent speech.

- o Characteristics which may be readily apparent to police officers:
    - o Delusional beliefs of events that are contrary to any evidence, such as being followed, poisoned, infidelity, etc.
    - o Hallucinations such as the reporting of hearing voices, smelling odors, odd tastes, visions, or unrealistic physical complaints.
    - o Incoherent or interrupted speech and thoughts.
    - o Disorganized behavior.

- Scene Management Techniques:
  - Remain calm and professional and give reassurance the person won't be harmed.
  - Involve more than one officer when possible.
  - Never leave the person unattended or alone.
  - Do not be fooled by a sudden return to reality. Stay alert and attentive.
  - Avoid quick and aggressive movements.
  - Do not argue or agree with delusions or hallucinations reported.
  - Make sure the person is not physically ill and involve medical personnel if warranted.
  - Involve mental health professionals as soon as practical.

Cannabis Intoxication

Cannabis intoxication may produce behavioral and psychological changes, and in some occasions may produce Substance Induced Hallucinations.

- o Characteristics which may be readily apparent to police officers:
    - o Impaired coordination.
    - o Anxiety
    - o Impaired judgement.
    - o Dry mouth.

- o Scene Management Techniques:
    - o Make sure the person is not physically ill.
    - o Involve trained medical personnel if warranted.
    - o Use simple sentences and speak calmly and clearly.
    - o Be patient.
    - o Avoid unnecessary touching.

Some States and jurisdictions allow detention for <u>Emergency Evaluation</u> persons

who present a danger to themselves or others due to <u>Substance Dependence</u> or addiction.

Cannabis Withdrawal

Cannabis withdrawal disorder occurs after a prolonged period of heavy use over a period of several weeks to months.

- o Characteristics which may be readily apparent to police officers:
    - o Anxiety
    - o Aggression
    - o Anger and irritability.
    - o Depression

- o Scene Management Techniques:
    - o Make sure the person is not physically ill.
    - o Involve trained medical personnel if necessary.
    - o Involve more than one officer when possible.
    - o Never leave the person unattended.

- Don't agitate the person or challenge them into action.
- Don't use intimidation, shout orders, or threaten the person.
- Avoid unnecessary touching.

Some States and jurisdictions allow detention for <u>Emergency Evaluation</u> persons who present a danger to themselves or others due to <u>Substance Dependence</u> or addiction.

Conduct Disorder

Conduct Disorder in an impulse control disorder in which the person frequently violates the rights of others and violates laws and rules. The disorder generally begins before 13 years of age. This conduct beyond age 18 is generally referred to as Antisocial Personality Disorder.

About 20 percent of youth ages 13 to 18 experience some type of mental illness in a given year. (NAMI)

- Characteristics which may be readily apparent to police officers:

- o Physical aggression involving cruelty to people or animals in which the person bullies or threatens, initiates physical fights and assaults, and may have used a weapon.
- o The person has committed robbery while confronting the victim.
- o They deliberately set fires or destroys property.
- o Deceitfulness or theft has been committed by the person.
- o Violations of age-appropriate rules such as smoking, drinking, truancy, and staying out all night despite parent's prohibition.
- o Their behavior is out of proportion to any provocation.

- o Scene Management Techniques:
  - o Involve two or more officers if available to reduce the amount of force if force is necessary.

- o Don't start out expecting a confrontation.
- o Help regain control of the scene.
- o Do not challenge them into confrontation or otherwise agitate the event.
- o Don't squabble or argue with family members present.
- o Ask unnecessary persons to leave the room.
- o Remain calm and professional.
- o Do not leave the person unattended or alone.

Delirium

Delirium is a mental disturbance that is a result of another medical condition, exposure to certain toxins, or substance abuse involving intoxication or withdrawal.

- o Characteristics which may be readily apparent to police officers:
  - o Inability to sustain attention.
  - o Deficits in memory and language abilities.

○ Disorientation*
○ Issue involving perception.

○ Scene Management Techniques:
- ○ Make sure the person is not physically ill and involve medical personnel if warranted.
- ○ Involve more than one officer when possible.
- ○ Never leave the person unattended or alone.
- ○ Do not be fooled by a sudden return to reality. Stay alert and attentive.
- ○ Avoid quick and aggressive movements.
- ○ Involve mental health professionals as soon as practical.

*Some States and jurisdictions allow detention for <u>Emergency Evaluation</u> persons who present a danger to themselves or others due to <u>Substance Dependence</u> or addiction.

Delusional Disorders

Delusional disorders involve a belief by someone that are contrary to any evidence. Delusional disorder differs from Schizophrenia and other psychotic episodes in that their behavior and ability to function normally is less impaired or noticeable.

- o Characteristics which may be apparent to police officers:
    - o Erotomania type of delusions is where the person believes that another person, usually of fame or higher status, is in love with them.
    - o Grandiose type of delusions is where the person believes they have some special talent or magical gift contrary to any evidence.
    - o Jealous type is where the person believes their spouse or lover is being unfaithful contrary to any evidence.

- Persecutory type where the person believes they are being followed or targeted in some manner, such as being poisoned, cheated, etc.
- Somatic type is where the person believes they have a physical ailment or condition, such as being infested with fleas or a disease contrary to any evidence.

- Scene Management Techniques:
  - Do not argue with or agree with delusions.
  - Be patient. Mental illnesses are biological brain diseases that you can't talk someone out of just like you can't talk someone out of kidney or liver diseases.
  - Maintain a calm and professional dialogue to bring the conversation back into reality.
  - Delusions do not go away by reasoning or demanding.

- o Involve mental health professionals as soon as practical.

Note: See the Case Study of Margret Mary Ray

Depressive Disorders (Major Depression)

Major depression is a feeling of sadness, guilt, and hopelessness usually out of proportion to the person's circumstances. Of particular importance to police officers, depression often involve suicidal thoughts and attempts. About 14.8 million Americans live with Major Depression.

- o Characteristics which may be readily apparent to police officers:
  - o Threats of suicide. *
  - o Attempts to commit suicide. *
  - o Depressed sad mood.
  - o Feelings of extreme worthlessness and guilt.
  - o Diminished memory.
  - o Diminished ability to concentrate or make decisions.

- o Scene Management Techniques:
    - o Take all threats of suicide seriously. *
    - o Be patient. Mental illnesses are biological brain diseases that you can't talk someone out of just like you can't talk someone out of kidney or liver diseases.
    - o Involve family members unless they are the root of the depression.
    - o Do not criticize or lecture the person.
    - o Do not lie or try to deceive the person.
    - o Involve mental health professionals as soon as practical.
    - o Don't agitate the person further.
    - o Comply with reasonable requests.
    - o Do not challenge the person into action or confrontation.

- Do not leave the person unattended or alone.

*Substantial threats or attempts to harm themselves may be cause for involuntary commitments.

Dissociative Identity Disorder (Multiple Personalities)

Dissociative Identity Disorder is a disruption of memory and identity, some of which is discussed in dissociative amnesia. Formerly known as Multiple Personalities, the event is rare but can come to the attention of police officers in cases in which there may be a lack of identity of an individual.

- Characteristics which may be readily apparent to police officers:
  - The presence of two or more distinct personalities.
  - Changes in mood, behavior, and memory.

- o Inability to recall important personal information and previous history.

- o Scene Management Techniques:
  - o Bring the behavior to the attention of mental health professionals as soon as possible.
  - o Give reassurance the person will not be harmed.
  - o Involve family members if possible.
  - o Don't argue or agree with their identity.
  - o Be patient. Mental illnesses are biological brain diseases that you can't talk someone out of just like you can't talk someone out of kidney or liver diseases.

Excited Delirium

Excited Delirium is not listed in the DSM-5 of the American Psychiatric Association or the American Medical Association as a mental or medical disorder but is widely recognized by the American College of Emergency Physicians and others.

Excited Delirium is still controversial and is most commonly associated with deaths at the hands of police officers during an arrest in which a taser is often used on the person.

The condition describes a series of events in which the person becomes extremely agitated, verbally or physically aggressive, and sweating profusely during physical restraint, leading to unconsciousness, cardiac failure, and death.

The body temperature of Adam Trammel was 104 degrees one hour after his death while was tased multiple times by police.

In some cases, the injection of Ketamine by paramedics to sedate the person can cause cardiac arrest as well.

- o Scene management techniques mirror those of schizophrenia, delirium, and hallucinations.

Note: See Case Studies of Adam Trammel, Daniel Prude, and Elijah McClain.

Hallucinations

Hallucinations are distortions in perception which, however, are clearly present to the individual experiencing one or more of them. Hallucinations are most commonly experienced in Schizophrenia Spectrum Disorders and other psychotic disorders.

- Characteristics which may be readily apparent to police officers:
    - Auditory hallucinations are the most common in which the person experiences hearing voices that are not present to others.
    - Visions are commonly associated with Substance Abuse Disorders or other medications.
    - Olfactory hallucinations involve the person reporting odd smells.
    - Gustatory hallucinations are where the person reports odd tastes.

- Tactile hallucinations involve claims by the person to have unrealistic physical complaints or bodily sensations.

Hallucinogen Intoxication

The use of hallucinogens creates a change in behavior and psychologically distressing symptoms in which there can be anxiety, depression, impaired judgement, and paranoia shortly after use*.
- Characteristics that may be readily apparent to police officers:
  - Paranoia
  - Perceptual hallucinations
  - Tremors
  - Blurred vision
  - Lack of coordination
  - Impaired judgement
  - Dilation of pupils
  - Profuse sweating
- Scene Management Techniques:
  - Involve more than one officer when possible.

o Make sure the person isn't physically ill.
o Don't bait the person into confrontation or crowd the person.
o Avoid unnecessary touching unless warranted for medical attention or arrest.
o Involve trained medical personnel as soon as practical.
o Give assurance the person will not be harmed

*Some States allow detention for <u>Emergency Evaluation</u> persons who present a danger to themselves or others due to <u>Substance Dependence</u> or addiction.

Hallucinogen Persisting Perception Disorder (Flashbacks)

Flashbacks involve re-experiencing the effects of hallucinogens, well after cessation from use and without current intoxication. *
o Characteristics that may be readily apparent to police officers:

- Paranoia
- Perceptual hallucinations
- Tremors
- Blurred vision
- Lack of coordination
- Impaired judgement
- Dilation of pupils
- Profuse sweating

- Scene Management Techniques:
  - Involve more than one officer when possible.
  - Make sure the person isn't physically ill.
  - Don't bait the person into confrontation or crowd the person.
  - Avoid unnecessary touching unless warranted for medical attention or arrest.
  - Involve trained medical personnel as soon as practical.
  - Give assurance the person will not be harmed

*Some States and jurisdictions allow detention for <u>Emergency Evaluation</u> persons who present a danger to themselves or others due to <u>Substance Dependence</u> or addiction.

Intellectual Disabilities

Intellectual disabilities are a group of disorders known as Neurodevelopmental Disorders that occur during development. They are also defined by levels of severity, those being, Mild, Moderate, Severe, and Profound.

- o Characteristics which may be apparent to police officers:
    - o Limited functioning in communications skills.
    - o Limited functioning in reasoning and judgement.
    - o Limited functioning in social skills.
    - o Mildly disabled persons can function adequately with

supervision in stressful situations.

- o Moderately disabled persons can adequately care for themselves but need supervision and guidance under stressful situations.
- o Severely disabled persons can partially help care for themselves under complete supervision.
- o Profoundly disabled persons have some communications skills but need complete care, supervision, and guidance.

- o Scene Management Techniques:
  - o BE PATIENT
  - o Involve mental health professionals as soon as practical, if necessary.
  - o Give assurance that they will not be harmed.
  - o Involve family members if available.

- Comply with reasonable requests.
- Remain calm and professional.
- Use simple and clear sentences.
- Do not shout orders or use intimidation.
- Avoid unnecessary touching or movements that may be interpreted as aggressive.

Some States and jurisdictions allow detention for <u>Emergency Evaluation</u> when a person is <u>Gravely Disabled</u> and unable to satisfy the need for basic care, such as food, shelter, and medical care.

Note: United States Public Law 111-256, known as Rosa's Law, replaces the terms mental retardation and mental impairment with Intellectual Disability or Intellectual Development Disorder.

Note: See Case Study of Death of Robert Ethan Saylor

Intermittent Explosive Disorder

Intermittent Explosive Disorder involves reoccurring aggressive outbursts that are uncontrollable by the individual. *
- o Characteristics which may be readily apparent to police officers:
    - o Verbal insults and tantrums resulting in arguments or fights.
    - o Physical aggression toward people, animals, and property.
    - o Outbursts involving injury to people, animals, or property.
    - o Their aggressive behavior is out of proportion to any provocations or circumstance.

- o Scene Management Techniques
    - o Remain calm and professional.
    - o Don't start out expecting a confrontation.
    - o Do not bait the person into a confrontation.
    - o Don't agitate the person further.

- o Don't leave the person unattended.
- o Don't criticize or lecture the person.
- o Avoid touching until warranted to control the scene or to arrest.

*Substantial threats or attempts to harm themselves or others may be cause for involuntary commitments.

Note: See Case Study of Eric Smith

Kleptomania

Kleptomania is an Impulse Disorder in which the person is unable to resist the urge or impulse to steal objects that the person doesn't need, or doesn't want, and is not done for monetary gain. Typically, the items stolen have little value. In many cases the person has the money or means to purchase the items stolen.

Opioid Intoxication

Opioid Intoxication involves a recent use of an opioid causing behavioral and psychological problems. *

- o Characteristics which may be readily apparent to police officers:
  - o Constriction of the pupils.
  - o Initial feelings of euphoria.
  - o Agitated or retarded motor skills.
  - o Drowsiness or coma.
  - o Slurred speech.
  - o Impaired memory.
  - o Inability to sustain attention.

- o Scene Management Techniques:
  - o Notify properly trained medical personnel as soon as practical.
  - o Make sure the person is not physically ill.
  - o Involve more than one officer when possible.
  - o Speak calmly and clearly using simple sentences.

- o Do not leave the person unattended.
- o Avoid any unnecessary touching.

*Some States and jurisdictions allow detention for <u>Emergency Evaluation</u> persons who present a danger to themselves or others due to <u>Substance Dependence</u> or addiction.

Oppositional Defiant Disorder

Oppositional Defiant Disorder is a pattern of irritable, argumentative, and defiant behavior which usually develops in childhood years from pre-school to adolescence. Oppositional Defiant Disorder is a forerunner to Conduct Disorder in many, but not all cases.
- o Characteristics which may be readily apparent to police officers:
  - o Loss of temper and anger out of proportion to any provocation or level of provocation presented.

- The child is often argumentative with adults and other authoritative figures.
- The child openly and actively defies rules and refuses to comply with requests from adults or authority.
- The child displays vindictiveness and blames others for their behavior and failures.

- Scene Management Techniques:
  - Remain calm and professional.
  - Help regain control of the scene.
  - Do not threaten or use sarcasm.
  - Involve family members unless they are a source of agitation.
  - Don't start out expecting a confrontation.
  - Do not challenge the child into a confrontation.
  - Don't agitate the child further.
  - Don't leave the child unattended.

- o Don't criticize or lecture the child.
- o Avoid touching until warranted to control the scene.

Note: See Case Study of Deputy Ben Fields, Richland County Sheriff's Office.

Panic Attacks

Panic Attacks are episodes of intense fear and anxiousness which may be associated with Agoraphobia, which is the fear of public places such as large, open, crowded spaces. They may also occur in closed spaces such as theaters or on public transportation. The behavior might bring the attention of police officers or medical personnel.
- o Characteristics which may be readily apparent to police officers:
  - o Trembling, shaking, or shortness of breath.
  - o Reports of chest pain, heart palpitations, or feelings of choking.

- Dizziness, light headedness, nausea, sweating.

- Scene Management Techniques:
    - Bring this to the attention of trained medical personnel as soon as practical.
    - Don't crowd; Give the person space.
    - Ask unnecessary persons to leave the area.
    - Never leave the person unattended.
    - Give assurance they will not be harmed.

Paraphilias – Abnormal Sexual Behavior

Paraphilic Disorders or paraphilias, are recurrent and intense sexually arousing fantasies or urges involving nonhuman objects, the suffering or humiliation of one's self or one's partner, or involving children and nonconsenting persons.

- Exhibitionism involves the recurring intense sexually arousing fantasies or urges to expose one's genitals.
- Fetishism involves the recurring intense sexually arousing fantasies or urges involving nonhuman objects, such as women's panties, shoes, etc.
- Frotteurism involves the recurring intense sexually arousing fantasies and urges involving the touching and rubbing against a nonconsenting person, usually in a crowded place or on public transportation.
- Pedophilia involves the recurring intense sexually arousing fantasies or urges involving sexual activity with prepubescent children.
- Sexual Masochism involves the recurring intense sexually arousing fantasies and urges and behaviors involving being beaten, humiliated, bound, or otherwise made to suffer by self-mutilation, bondage, paddling, whipping, etc., and in extreme cases oxygen deprivation.

- Sexual Sadism involves the recurring intense sexually arousing fantasies and urges involving acts in which the psychological or physical suffering of the partner is sexually exciting. Real acts of bondage, beating, paddling, whipping, cutting or oxygen deprivation describe a few behaviors.
- Voyeurism involves the recurring intense sexually arousing fantasies and urges involving the act of observing nonconsenting and unsuspecting persons naked, partially disrobed, or engaged in sexual activity.

Phencyclidine (PCP) Intoxication

Phencyclidine Intoxication involves recent use of PCP leading to a change in behavior which includes impulsive and unpredictable action such as physical assaults, belligerence, and impaired judgement. *

- Characteristics which may be readily apparent to police officers:
  - Belligerent language.

- Aggression. *
- Vertical or horizontal nystagmus.
- Reduced numbness to pain.
- Seizures or coma.

- Scene Management Techniques:
  - Involve more than one officer when possible.
  - Don't bait the person into confrontation or crowd the person.
  - Avoid unnecessary touching unless warranted for arrest.
  - Involve trained medical personnel as soon as practical.

*Substantial threats or attempts to harm others may be cause for involuntary commitments.

Some States and jurisdictions allow detention for <u>Emergency Evaluation</u> persons who present a danger to themselves or others due to <u>Substance Dependence</u> or addiction.

Posttraumatic Stress Disorder (PTSD)

PTSD is a complex disorder involving many different characteristics some of which are not readily apparent to a police officer. However, there are going to be characteristics of behavior present that occur in other disorders, such as Depression and Anxiety.

PTSD may occur after witnessing or be exposed to a traumatic event involving death, serious injuries, sexual assault, or frequent and repeated exposure to details of traumatic events. The exposure results in reoccurring and involuntary memories or dreams of the event which causes the person to avoid conversations, people, places, situations, or objects associated with the event.

The person may experience feelings of guilt or blame, shame, worthlessness, detachment from family and others, and diminished interest in activities. PTSD is a leading cause of suicide in veterans.

- o Characteristics which may be readily apparent to police officers include:

- Depression.
- Angry outbursts.
- Irritability.
- Aggression towards others with little provocation. *
- Memory loss.
- Gaps in memory about the experience witnessed.
- Self-destructive behavior. *
- Attempts or threats of suicide. *

- Scene Management Techniques:
  - Involve more than one officer when possible.
  - Involve trained mental health professionals as soon as practical.
  - Don't start out expecting confrontation or agitate the person further.
  - Don't crowd the person or challenge them into a confrontation.
  - Comply with reasonable requests.

- o Don't use intimidation or shout orders.
- o Avoid patronizing or authoritative statements toward the person.
- o Avoid quick movements or decisions that may appear aggressive.
- o Take all suicide threats seriously. *

*Substantial threats or attempts to harm themselves or others may be cause for involuntary commitments.

Note: See Case Study of Nikkolas Lookabill and Vancouver, WA, Police

Pyromania

Pyromania is an Impulse Control Disorder involving the intentional setting of fires on more than one occasion and not for revenge, anger, protest, concealing another crime, insurance fraud, or economic gain.

Pyromaniacs have a fascination with fire, fire paraphernalia, the setting of fires and observing burning sites.

Schizophrenia Spectrum Disorders

Schizophrenia and other psychotic disorders share similar characteristics that includes Delusional Disorder and Brief Psychotic Disorder (both previously listed), Schizoaffective Disorder, Schizophreniform, and Schizotypal Personality Disorder.

While these may differ in duration and severity, they do share common traits.
- Characteristics which may be readily apparent to police officers:
  - Delusional thinking.
  - Auditory hallucination, i.e., hearing voices.
  - Command hallucinations in which they report voices telling them to act.
  - Hallucinations involving smells, bodily functions, vision, and taste.

- Agitated behavior.
- Abnormal or rigid postures of the body and face.
- Excessive activity.
- Unusual or repetitive rituals.
- Ideas shift abruptly.
- Words or phrases not logically connected in speech.
- Repetitive speech.
- Lack of emotional response.

- Scene Management Techniques:
    - Involve more than one officer when possible.
    - Involve trained mental health professionals as soon as practical.
    - Never leave the person unattended.
    - Be patient. Use simple and clear sentences.
    - Give assurance they won't be harmed.
    - Don't be fooled by a sudden return to reality.

- o Don't argue or agree with delusion or hallucinations.
- o Comply with reasonable requests.
- o Don't shout orders or intimidate the person.
- o Avoid unnecessary touching.

Some States and jurisdictions allow detention for Emergency Evaluation when a person is Gravely Disabled and unable to satisfy the need for basic care, such as food, shelter, and medical care.

Note: See Case Studies of James Boyd, Deborah Danner, Charleena Lyles, and Iman Morales

Substance Induced Disorders

Substance Induced or Substance Abuse Disorders include Delirium, Dementia, Amnesia, and Psychotic Disorders. They exhibit the same characteristics as previously listed under these included disorders, except they are a result of intoxication or withdrawal.
*

Over 9 Million adults have both mental disorders and substance addictions.

- o Characteristics that may be readily apparent to police officers include:
    - o Inability to focus or maintain attention
    - o Disorientation and perceptual distortions
    - o Deficits in language use and memory.
    - o Failures to recognize people or objects.
    - o Failure to recall personal information about themselves.
    - o Deficits in motor skills.
    - o Hallucinations.
    - o Delusions.

- o Scene Management Techniques:
    - o Involve more than one officer when possible.
    - o Involve trained medical personnel when practical

- Never leave the person unattended.
- Remain calm and professional.
- Don't challenge them into confrontation.
- Do not crowd the person.
- Don't agitate the person further.
- Do not rely on presenting your weapon to control the scene.
- Do not threaten the person, shout orders, or use intimidation.
- Do not argue or agree with delusions or hallucinations.

*Some States and jurisdictions allow detention for <u>Emergency Evaluation</u> persons who present a danger to themselves or others due to <u>Substance Dependence</u> or addiction.

Note: See Case Study of Alton Sterling and Baton Rouge Police Department.

Suicide Behavior

There are many predictors of suicide in addition to depression. About 90% of those who commit suicide had one or more mental disorders. Veterans represent about 20% of suicides annually. (NAMI)
- o Suicide Risk Factors:
    - o Anorexia and Bulimia
    - o Alcoholism
    - o Bipolar Disorder
    - o Depressive Disorders
    - o Dissociative Amnesia and Identity Disorders
    - o Panic Disorders
    - o Substance Abuse
    - o Schizophrenia Spectrum Disorders
    - o Posttraumatic Stress Disorder.
    - o History of Suicide Attempts

- o Scene Management Techniques:
    - o TAKE ALL THREATS OF SUICIDE SERIOUSLY.
    - o Never leave the person alone.

- Help gain control of the scene.
- Involve trained mental health professionals as soon as practical.
- Be patient. These situations may take a long time to resolve successfully.
- Try to determine what circumstance or event led to this particular moment and try to find a solution.
- Remain calm, professional and give assurances they won't be harmed.
- Do not challenge them to act.
- Avoid sarcastic, authoritative, or patronizing statements.
- Comply with reasonable requests.
- Don't make promises they know you can't produce.
- Do not try to lie to or deceive the person.

*Substantial threats or attempts to harm themselves may be cause for involuntary commitments.

Note: See case study of Dustin Pigeon

- o Myths Versus Facts About Suicide

    - o Myth - People who threaten suicide are looking for attention and less likely to commit suicide than those who never discuss their intentions.
    - o Fact – Most people who commit suicide had communicated their intentions, even as subtly saying "you would be better off if I were dead" or "you're not going to have to worry about me much longer" or gave away prize possessions.

    - o Myth – Suicide attempts are committed by those wanting attention.

o Fact – Most people who commit suicide have previously attempted suicide or have made a plan to do so.

o Myth – Only people of low social or economic status will commit suicide.

o Fact – According to a study by Dr. Deepika Tanwar and presented to the American Psychological Association in 2018, doctors die by suicide at the highest rate. Dentists and police officers are consistently near the top of those who commits suicide at a higher rate.

o Myth – Only people who are depressed or insane will commit suicide.

o Fact – About half suffer from depression and most are completely in touch with reality. Alcohol, antidepressants, and opioids contribute to death by suicide along with several other mental disorders.

- o Myth – Depressed people whose emotional state improves are less at risk for suicide.
- o Fact – Many people who commit suicide simply believe they have run out of options. Once they decide how and when they will commit suicide, their outlook may very well appear happier.

- o Myth – Motives for suicide are easily established.
- o Fact – The reason may never be known. Recent upsets may have been the 'straw that broke the camel's back' so to speak, but the reasons are more complex than a single event. Most do not leave a note.

- o Myth – Elderly people are at much less risk of committing suicide.
- o Fact – According to the National Institute of Mental Health, elderly males over 65 years of age make up the highest rate of death by suicide.

Suicide by Cop

Suicide by Cop is a term used to define the completion of suicide by confronting police officers and prompting or forcing them to use deadly force against one's self.
- o Characteristics which may be readily apparent to police officers:
  - o Presentation and threatening the use of a deadly weapon.
  - o Intentional refusal to comply with officers' instructions.
  - o Challenging police to take deadly action or use deadly force.
  - o Threats of suicide or harm to others. *

- ○ Scene Management Techniques
  - ○ Take all threats of suicide seriously. *
  - ○ Never leave the person alone.
  - ○ Involve trained mental health professionals if possible and time permits.
  - ○ Be patient.
  - ○ Remain calm and professional.
  - ○ Do not challenge them into action or confrontation.
  - ○ Do not criticize or lecture the person.
  - ○ Avoid sarcastic, authoritative, or patronizing statements.
  - ○ Do not try to lie to or deceive the person.

*Substantial threats or attempts to themselves may be cause for involuntary commitments.

Note: See Case Studies of Nikkolas Lookabill and Micah Jester

Managing Mental Illness among Police Officers

Police officers are not immune from mental disorders. While officers are often screened during the application and hiring process, the onset of various mental disorders can occur well into adulthood.

The following disorders are the most common to occur because of their occupation.

- Major Depression
- Posttraumatic Stress Disorder
- Acute Stress Disorder
- Anxiety Disorders
- Substance and Alcohol Disorders

Behavior that is most recognizable to police managers:

- Increase use of alcohol or substances.
- Depressed mood.
- Hypervigilance
- Impulsive risk taking or self-destructive behavior.

- Sleep disorders.
- Abrupt weight loss or gain.
- Absenteeism
- Failure to complete assignments.
- Uncontrolled anger and irritability.

Contributing factors:

- Unfavorable court decisions
- Ineffective corrections system
- Unfavorable media accounts
- Unfavorable attitudes from the public
- Special assignments
- Shift work
- Moonlighting
- Disciplinary issues
- Use of deadly force
- Poor supervision
- Inadequate resources

Involuntary Mental Commitment Procedures in Each State (Alphabetically)

The laws of the United States allow two reasons to take away the rights of mentally ill individuals by law enforcement officers in civil matters.

With respect to those with mentally illness both reasons are the same, that is, if a person is an immediate danger to themselves or others due to mental illness, those persons can be involuntarily committed to a mental health facility after due process is provided.

What defines immediate danger and due process differ from state to state. Moreover, what is black and white in the state code may not match the practices of local mental health hygiene officers or commissioners in different jurisdictions.

It is imperative that police officers not only know the state laws but also the process that the local county courts in each individual jurisdiction have outlined. Police in every state may detain for evaluation someone who is mentally ill and pose a danger to themselves or others, however, many states require a prior application process or written order.

There are various stages of probable cause hearings and evidence that must be presented in order to involuntarily take someone's freedom in either case.

The difference from criminal cases is that someone who is detained for involuntary commitment is going for treatment and not incarceration in jail. Another difference is the U.S. Supreme Court ruled in the 1975 case of Dixon v. Weinberger, and other cases, that the person has the right to be treated in the "least restrictive environment."

Below are involuntary commitment procedures of each state in which police officers may detain a mentally ill person under emergency circumstances for mental health evaluations and treatment.

It is important that police officers review their state laws as there may be legislative changes from year to year and consult with local officials for changes in practices.

Alabama Title §22-52-91(a) – police officers who have reasonable cause that a person meets criteria for commitment shall contact a community mental health officer who must have clear and convincing evidence the person is mentally ill; poses a real and present threat of substantial harm to themselves or others; will continue to experience mental distress if not treated; is unable to make rational treatment decisions on their own.

Alaska Title §47.30.705(a) – a peace officer may take a person into custody when they have probable cause to believe an individual is gravely disabled or mentally ill and likely to cause serious harm to themselves or others of such immediate nature that considerations do not allow initiation of involuntary commitment procedures.

Arizona Title §36-525(B) – a police officer may take into custody a person they have probable cause to believe, based on their observation, is a danger to themselves or a danger to others, and immediate detention or hospitalization is necessary to prevent serious harm to themselves or others.

Arkansas Title §20-47-210 – an individual may be detained for evaluation if the officer witnesses or receives credible information that the person is an imminent danger of causing death or serious harm to themselves or to others.

California Code Section §5150 – an individual may be detained by a peace officer for evaluation if they are mentally ill and a danger to themselves or to others, or are gravely disabled.

Colorado §27-65-105 – a person may be detained by a peace officer for evaluation when found to have a mental illness and appear to be an imminent danger to themselves or others, or appears to be gravely disabled.

Connecticut Sec. §17a-503 – a person may be detained if a police officer has reasonable cause to believe that the person has psychiatric disabilities and is dangerous to themselves or others, or gravely disabled, and in need of immediate care and treatment.

Delaware Title 16 §5122 (12)(b) – a person may be detained if they are mentally ill and a danger to themselves or others upon observation of a peace officer or credentialed mental health screener.

District of Columbia Title §21-521 – officers authorized to make arrests who have reason to believe that a person is mentally ill, and likely to injure themselves or others if not immediately detained, may take that person into custody for evaluation at a proper facility.

Florida Chapter §394.463(2)(a)– a person may be detained by police for an involuntary examination if there is a substantial likelihood that without treatment the person will cause serious harm to themselves or others in the near future, as evidenced by recent behavior.

Georgia Title §37-3-32(a) – a person may be detained by police upon probable cause when there is an imminent danger to themselves or others, evidenced by recent overt acts or expressed threats of violence, or they are unable to care for their physical health and safety so as to create an imminently life-endangering crisis.

Hawaii § 334-59(a)(1) – police officers with reason to believe a person may be mentally ill or suffering from substance abuse, and the person is imminently dangerous to themselves or others, shall call for assistance from the mental health emergency worker designated by the director. Officers may take into custody and transport to a facility any person threatening or attempting suicide.

Idaho Title §66-326(1) – a person may be detained by a peace officer if there is reason to believe the person is gravely disabled due to mental illness; or the person's continued liberty poses a danger to themselves or others, as evidenced by a threat of substantial physical harm.

Illinois Section §405 ILCS 5/3-606 – a person may be detained by a peace officer for evaluation when, because of mental illness, there is a reasonable expectation of danger to self or others; they are unable to provide basic physical needs as to guard against physical harm; they refuse or fail to adhere to treatment; there is a reasonable expectation they will suffer mental or emotional deterioration and become dangerous or unable to provide basic needs.

Indiana Title §12-26-7-2(b) – allows police officers to file an emergency application for detention of persons who are mentally ill and a danger to themselves or others; or gravely disabled and in need of immediate restraint.

Iowa Code §229.22(2a) – allows for a person to be taken into custody by police if there are reasonable grounds to believe the person is mentally ill and likely to cause physical injury to themselves or others if not immediately detained; or due to intoxication or substance abuse has threatened, attempted, or inflicted physical self-harm or harm to others.

Kansas §59-2953(a) – allows for a person to be taken into custody by police for evaluation who is mentally ill and because of mental illness has a reason to believe is likely to cause harm to themselves or others if not taken into custody.

Kentucky §202a.041(1) – a person may be detained for evaluation by a peace officer who has reason to believe is mentally ill and presents a danger or threat of danger of substantial physical harm to themselves or others.

Louisiana §28:53-L (1) – allows police to take into custody any person who is observed by them to be mentally ill and has reason to believe the person is acting in a manner dangerous to themselves or others, or is gravely disabled, and is in need of immediate hospitalization to protect themselves or others from such harm.

Maine Title 34B- § 3862– allows police to detain someone upon probable cause that a person who is mentally ill and presents a threat of imminent and substantial danger to the themselves or others.

Maryland Code §10-622 – allows police to detain and file a petition on a person they have personally observed to have a mental disorder and presents a danger to the life or safety of themselves or others.

Massachusetts Chapter 123, § 12 – In the absence of physicians and other qualified persons, police may restrain a person for evaluation who is mentally ill and a substantial risk of physical harm to themselves or others that is evidenced by threat or attempts of suicide, or evidence of homicidal or other violent behavior, or behavior that places others in reasonable fear of violence or physical harm.

Michigan §330.1427(1) – peace officers may take into custody persons they reasonably believe are mentally ill, and as a result, can reasonably be expected within the near future to intentionally or unintentionally injure themselves or others; and who has engaged in acts or made significant threats that support the expectation of causing harm.

Minnesota §253B.05(2) – police may take into custody a person they have reason to believe, through direct personal observation or upon reliable information of the person's recent behavior and history, that the person is mentally ill, or developmentally disabled, and in danger of injuring themselves or others if not immediately detained.

Mississippi §41-21-67 – a designated professional who has reason to believe that a person poses an immediate substantial likelihood of physical harm to themselves or others or is gravely disabled and unable to care for themselves, may hold the person or may admit the person and treat the person without a warrant for 72 hours.

Missouri Statute 632.305(3) – police officers may initiate emergency custody of a person they have reasonable cause to believe is mentally ill, and that the likelihood of the person causing serious harm to themselves or others is imminent unless taken into custody immediately.

Montana Code §53-21-129 (1) – police officers may take any person who appears to be mentally ill and presents an imminent danger of death or bodily injury to themselves or others immediately for emergency evaluation by a professional.

Nebraska Statute §71-919(1) – police officers who have probable cause to believe a person is mentally ill and a risk of serious harm to themselves or others as evidenced by recent attempts or threats of suicide; a risk of serious harm to other persons as evidenced by recent violent acts or threats; placing someone in reasonable fear of violence; or evidence of an inability to provide themselves with basic needs leading to harm, may be taken into custody for immediate evaluation.

Nevada §433A.160 – police officers without a warrant may take a person alleged to be mentally ill into custody if based on personal observations have probable cause to believe the person is mentally ill and likely to harm themselves or others if not detained for evaluation.

New Hampshire Statute §135-C:28 – police officers who observe a person they believe is mentally ill, has inflicted or threatened to inflict bodily harm to themselves, or attempts suicide; has inflicted, attempted to inflict, or threaten to inflict serious bodily harm on another, may be taken into custody.

New Jersey Statute §30:4-27-6 – police officers shall immediately take into custody and commit to treatment, persons they have reasonable cause to believe from their own personal observations are mentally ill, dangerous to themselves, or dangerous to others or property.

New Mexico Statute §43-1-10(A) – police officers may detain for emergency mental health examinations persons they have reason to believe attempted suicide; or based on observations and have reasonable grounds to believe that the person is mentally ill and presents a danger of serious harm to themselves or others and immediate detention is necessary to prevent harm.

New York Code §9.41 – police officers may take any person into custody for mental examinations that appears to be mentally ill and is conducting themselves in a manner in which they are likely to cause harm to themselves or others.

North Carolina Statute §122C-262(a) – police officers may detain and immediately transport to a facility subject for inpatient commitment, any person who has attempted or threatened suicide, self-mutilation, or has inflicted, attempted to inflict, or threatened to inflict serious bodily harm on another.

North Dakota Code §25-03. 1-25.1 – peace officers who have reasonable cause to believe that an individual requires treatment due to mental illness or chemical dependence, and if not treated there exists a serious risk of harm to themselves, others, or property, may detain that person for emergency evaluation.

Ohio §5122.10 – police officers may take someone into custody if they have reason to believe the person is mentally ill; and a substantial risk of harming themselves by evidence of threats or attempts of suicide or other means; or a substantial risk of harm to others as evidenced by recent homicidal or violent behavior or threats that would place someone in reasonable fear of injury.

Oklahoma §5-207 (B) – officers may take someone into protective custody who they reasonably believe is mentally ill, or drug or alcohol dependent; and because of such, poses a substantial risk of immediate physical harm through threats or attempts of suicide; harm to others evidenced by violent behavior directed toward them; or has placed someone in reasonable fear of serious injury by serious and immediate threats.

Oregon §426.228(1) – a peace officer may take into custody a person who the officer has probable cause to believe is dangerous to themselves or to any other person and is in need of immediate care, custody, or treatment for mental illness.

Pennsylvania §7302(a) – a person may be subjected to involuntary emergency examination or treatment, without a warrant upon application by authorized persons, who is severely mentally disabled, and in need of immediate treatment, and poses a clear and present danger of harm to themselves or others.

Rhode Island §40.1-5-7(a)(1) – in absence of a physician, a police officer who believes a person is a substantial risk to themselves by threats or attempts of suicide; or a substantial risk to others as evidenced by homicidal or other violent behavior; or a substantial risk of harm to themselves by behavior which has created a grave, clear, and present risk to their physical health and safety, may make an emergency application for evaluation.

South Carolina §44-13-05 – a law enforcement officer who observes a mentally ill or chemically dependent person conducting themselves in a manner they believe poses a likelihood of serious harm to self or others, may be taken into protective custody and transported to a mental health facility.

South Dakota §27A-10-3 – a peace officer may apprehend a person they have probable cause to believe requires emergency intervention because they are severely mentally ill and a danger of harming themselves or others.

Tennessee §33-6-402 – a police officer may take a mentally ill person into custody if they have reason to believe the person has threatened or attempted suicide; or inflicts bodily harm on others; or has threatened or attempted homicide or other violent behavior; or has placed others in reasonable fear of violent behavior and physical harm; or the person is unable to avoid severe impairment of injury from specific risks.

Texas §573.001(a) – a peace officer may take a person into custody without a warrant if they have reason to believe the person is mentally ill, and because of illness there is a substantial risk of serious harm to themselves or others.

Utah §62A-15-629(2) – a peace officer who observes a person involved in behavior that gives probable cause to believe the person is mentally ill, and there is a substantial likelihood of serious harm to the person or others because of the mental illness, may take the person into protective custody.

Vermont Title 18, §7505 (a) – in an emergency, a police officer may restrain a person who through personal observation there exists reasonable grounds to believe the person is in need of treatment and presents an immediate risk of serious injury to themselves or others if not restrained.

Virginia §37.2-808(G) – a police officer, based on his own observations or reliable reports of others that a person is mentally ill, and there is a substantial likelihood the person will cause physical harm to self or others as evidenced by recent behavior causing, attempting or threatening harm, may take the person into custody.

Washington §71.05.153(2) – a police officer may take or cause to be taken into custody a person who as a result of a mental illness presents an imminent likelihood of serious harm to themselves or others, or causing substantial damage to the property of others, or is in imminent danger because of being gravely disabled.

West Virginia – §27-5-2(a) – any adult person with reason to believe a person is mentally ill, and the person may cause serious physical harm to themselves or others if allowed to remain at liberty, may make application for involuntary commitment.

Wisconsin §51.15(1)(a) – police may detain a mentally ill person if they have reason to believe there is a substantial probability of physical harm to themselves as evidenced by recent threats or attempts at suicide or bodily harm; or a probability of physical harm to others as evidenced by recent homicidal or violent acts or placing someone in reasonable fear of violence and serious harm as evidenced by recent acts, attempts, or threats to do physical harm.

Wyoming §25-10-109(a) – mentally ill persons may be detained who police officers have reasonable cause to believe there is evidence of a substantial probability the person will physically harm themselves by threats or attempts of suicide or serious bodily injury; or there is a substantial probability of physical harm to others by recent homicidal acts, attempts or threats of other violent acts; or attempts or threats of violence that places someone in reasonable fear of serious physical harm.

Use of Force in Civil Commitments and Non-criminal Behavior

In the case of the Estate of Ronald Armstrong *v.* Village of Pinehurst, the U.S. Court of Appeals for the Fourth Circuit outlined several guidelines defining the use of force in a mental commitment after the death of Armstrong due to the actions of police officers enforcing a mental commitment order.

- o When encountering an unarmed mentally ill person who is non-threatening, officers must de-escalate the application of force downward.
- o When no crime is committed, the use of force weighs heavily in favor of the mentally ill person.
- o Officers need to consider the mental illness, particularly when the person is unarmed.
- o When taking a mentally ill person into custody because they pose a danger to

themselves, any force causing harm is contrary to the mission.

o The use of force should be analyzed based on what the person is doing each time force is applied.

o The use of a Taser is a serious use of force.

o Each time a Taser is used on the same person more than once must be viewed separately as to what the person was doing each time the Taser is implemented.

o A Taser is an unreasonable response to resistance that does not risk immediate danger.

o Non-violent resistance to being handcuffed when outnumbered by officers does not equate to a risk of immediate danger.

o Erratic behavior or mental illness does not necessarily create a safety risk.

o Physical resistance does not automatically equal immediate danger.

o Non-compliance with orders does not equal immediate danger.

○ A subject clinging to a pole and refusing to move does not constitute immediate danger so severe that the officers have to cause harm to the person they are protecting from harm.

Note: See the Case Study of Armstrong v. Village of Pinehurst

Case Studies

Use of Force
Armstrong v. The Village of Pinehurst

On April 23, 2011, Ronald Armstrong was taken to the hospital by his sister who feared for his safety because he was poking holes in his legs "to let the air out." Armstrong suffered from Schizophrenia and Bipolar Disorder and had stopped taking his medications.

After arriving at the hospital, the emergency room physician deemed he was a danger to himself. After the doctor left the examination room to begin preparing involuntary commitment orders, Armstrong became frightened and walked away from the hospital. Hospital security guards observed him on the hospital grounds and call the Pinehurst Police Department for assistance.

When police arrived, Armstrong was walking in traffic on a busy road in front of the hospital. Officers were able to coax him out of traffic and onto the hospital lawn where he began eating grass and dandelions. Additionally, he began lighting cigarettes and then extinguishing them by placing them against his tongue. Eventually, Armstrong was surrounded by three police officers and two security guards. His sister was also present as they waited on word that the commitment papers had been signed and issued by the physician.

Once Armstrong became aware the commitment papers had been issued, he wrapped his arms around a sign post and refused to let go. After officers tried negotiating with Armstrong to let go with no success, a Taser was used for pain compliance purposes five times over a two-minute period with no effect.

The three officers and two security guards then physically removed him from the post and laid him on his stomach with an officer placing his knee in Armstrong's back so his hands and feet could be handcuffed. Armstrong's sister then noticed her brother had stopped moving and was turning blue. She asked officers the to check him.

The officers turned Armstrong over onto his back and found he was no longer breathing and called for an ambulance. Armstrong was transported back to the hospital emergency room and was pronounced dead upon arrival.

A lawsuit was filed by the family. The case was moved to federal court and dismissed by the district court judge. The family appealed the dismissal to the Fourth Circuit who overturned the lower U.S. District Court and ruled that excessive force had been used in this case.

Use of Force - Failure to Train
Quintonio LeGrier and Chicago Police Department

Quintonio LeGrier began experiencing signs of mental illness while attending college in the fall of 2015. After several encounters with the campus police in which he claimed he was god, from outer space, and other bizarre statements, he was committed to a mental facility and released. He returned to his father's apartment for the semester break.

On December 26, 2015, LeGrier was in a psychological episode causing his father to barricade himself in his bedroom. A Chicago police officer responded to an apartment building regarding Quintonio LeGrier who had called 911 on three occasions demanding police be sent to his address. Each time he would call, the 911 dispatcher would disconnect him because LeGrier would not state the problem. Police officers were only sent after Quintonio's father called 911 stating he was fearing for his safety and that his son was mentally ill.

The dispatcher didn't inform the responding officers of the previous calls or the likelihood the person was mentally ill. When the officer arrived, he was met at the door by Bettie Jones who lived on the first floor. As Jones directed the officer upstairs, LeGrier suddenly appeared coming down the stairs with a baseball bat. The officer shot through the open doorway multiple times killing both LeGrier and Bettie Jones.

The families of LeGrier and Jones filed a lawsuit against the officer and the City of Chicago.

The officer filed a countersuit against the LeGrier estate claiming he had initiated the deadly incident, the 911 dispatcher for failing to provide adequate information, and the Chicago Police Department for failing to properly train him in mental health issues.

Later while the department was under a consent decree it was ruled that the officer and 911 personnel failed to request the department's emergency response team, the dispatcher failed to provide the officer adequate information, and the department failed to provide adequate training regarding mental illness.

Duty to Warn
Tarasoff v. University of California Medical Center

Tatiana Tarasoff was a student at the University of California at Berkley who had befriended and briefly dated another student from India named Prosenjit Poddar. After the relationship ended, Poddar underwent a severe emotional crisis. Tarasoff left campus for a long college break shortly after the affair.

Meanwhile, Poddar decided to seek psychological help at the university's medical center. During one visit, he confided in his doctor that he intended to kill Tarasoff. Dr. Moore diagnosed Poddar with acute and severe Paranoid Schizophrenia and asked campus police to detain him and recommended an involuntary commitment.

Poddar was detained but not committed as he appeared rational according to mental health officials who examined him. No university officials, campus police officials, or medical center staff notified Tarasoff of the threats. Tarasoff returned to the university, unaware of the threats made against her by Poddar. Several weeks after she returned to her dormitory, Poddar carried out his plan to commit murder by stabbing Tarasoff multiple times.

Tarasoff's parents sued the university for failing to warn their daughter of the credible threats. The California Supreme Court ruled that officials had a duty to warn Tarasoff and the circumstances outweighed any confidentiality or privacy privileges Poddar had with the medical center or others.

Schizophrenia
Iman Morales and the New York Police Department
Use of a Taser

On September 28, 2008, Iman Morales was observed running naked through the halls of the apartment building where he lived in New York City. Morales suffered from Schizophrenia and lived alone in his second story apartment.

A neighbor familiar with Morales and his mental illness called the man's mother to have her come to the apartment building and intervene. When she arrived a short time later, Morales was in possession of a long fluorescent light bulb which he would swing at people who tried to approached him. His mother was unable to coax him back inside the apartment, so she called the New York Police Department.

When officers from the Emergency Response Team headed by Lt. Michael Pigott arrived, Morales ran back into his apartment and climbed onto a ledge outside of his window. Morales was standing on a ledge about 10 feet from the sidewalk, and as officers tried to reach him, he would swing the glass tube at them.

After negotiating with him for a lengthy period of time, Lt. Pigott ordered one of his officers to shoot Morales with a taser gun. Morales immediately dropped forward head first onto the sidewalk in what one witness described as a "dead man fall." He died at the scene.

Lt. Pigott was placed on administrative duties and relinquished his duty weapon pending an investigation into the use of a Taser in those circumstances. Fearing the outcome of the internal investigation, Pigott drove to his former precinct station the following week where he knew he could retrieve a handgun in a locker and committed suicide on his 42nd birthday.

Schizoaffective Disorder
James Boyd and the Albuquerque Police Department

On March 16, 2014, the Albuquerque police were called to the foothills of the Sandia Mountain to assist two Open Space officers who were trying to remove a homeless man who was illegally camping.

James Matthew Boyd suffered from Schizoaffective Disorder which is defined as having Schizophrenia and a mood disorder such as depression. He had been camping in the area for about a month, and a complaint after he had confronted a nearby resident.

Two officers had approached Boyd when he suddenly produced two pocket knives and threatened them, resulting in a standoff.

Eventually, a total of 19 officers from the Albuquerque Police Department and New Mexico State Police responded and began negotiating with Boyd to surrender. Boyd made bizarre statements that he was on a Special Forces mission, and he could have all the officers killed with one phone call, along with other statements indicating he was mentally ill. One of the officers had dealt with Boyd in the past on other calls.

After lengthy negotiations, Boyd agreed to put his knives in his pocket. He picked his camping gear up and started walking down the hillside. After taking a couple of steps, an officer yelled "bang him" at which time a flash bang was used to distract Boyd. Another officer fired a Taser gun with no effect. Simultaneously, a K-9 was released on Boyd who was startled by the events and again pulled out his pocket knives and turned to go back up the hill.

At this point two officers shot Boyd six times. He fell face down on the ground, but was still breathing and holding the two knives. Another officer then shot Boyd with multiple bean bag charges from a shotgun.

Boyd was transported to a hospital where surgeons amputated one arm, removed his spleen, and part of his colon and one lung. He died several hours later after surgery.

The shooting was ruled as a criminal homicide by the medical examiner, and the two police officers who shot Boyd were charged with murder. The trial ended in a hung jury with nine jurors voting to acquit the officers, therefore, the case was not retried.

A lawsuit filed by the family resulted in a $5 million settlement from the Albuquerque Police Department.

Schizophrenia
Deborah Danner and NYPD

On October 18, 2016, NYPD officers were called to the apartment of Deborah Danner by residents who saw her acting erratically. Danner, 66 years old, was well-known to the officers as suffering from schizophrenia, and they had been to her apartment on other occasions.

Danner was found in her bedroom wielding a pair of scissors. An officer who arrived first went in the room with other officers behind him and was able to talk her into putting the scissors down. The officer then decided to rush her before she was able to pick up the scissors again, but she picked up a baseball bat and approached the officer as if to start swinging. The officer then shot her twice, killing her.

There were conflicting accounts of whether or not Danner was swinging the bat. One officer testified that she was not swinging the bat. The officer was placed on leave for violations of policy including not waiting on the Emergency Services Unit and other policy violations. He was later charged with Second Degree Murder, but was acquitted in a non-jury trial by a judge's ruling.

The judge ruled that the officer violated policy and had escalated the situation, but that even though he created the dangerous situation, he still had the right to use lethal force to protect himself.

Antisocial Personality Disorder
Jeffrey Dahmer and the Milwaukee Police Department

Jeffrey Dahmer was the infamous serial killer who preyed on homosexual men who he would drug and later kill. He reportedly stored body parts in his refrigerator and would cannibalize his victims. He was eventually caught and convicted and sent to prison where he was murdered by an inmate.

There was disagreement about whether or not Dahmer was a sociopath, but Dahmer exhibited those traits of showing no anxiety, remorse or guilt, even when confronted by police officers in Milwaukee.

Prior to being detected as a killer and arrested, Dahmer picked up a victim and took him back to his home where he drugged him and performed oral sex on the 14-year-old Asian boy. Dahmer then drilled a small hole in the boy's head and injected acid to further disable him.

Dahmer left his apartment for a little while and returned to find the naked boy sitting on the street corner and being attended to by 3 women who had called the police. The victim could not speak English. Upon arrival of police officers, Dahmer very calmly and with no anxiety explained to the two officers that the boy was his 19-year-old boyfriend who had too much to drink leading to an argument. Dahmer offered to take the boy back to his apartment, and the officers agreed in spite of protests from the three women who pointed out that the male was bleeding from his rectum.

Dahmer displayed no signs of anxiety that a normal person would while confronted by police. Dahmer's calmness and demeanor convinced the officers that he was telling the truth and one officer told the women to "butt out" and not interfere. Dahmer took the boy back to his apartment and injected him with a fatal dose of acid in the brain.

Dahmer went on to kill four more victims before he was arrested. The officers were fired and the city settled a subsequent lawsuit.

Developmental and Intellectual Disorder
Robert Ethan Saylor

On January 12, 2013, Robert Ethan Saylor went to a movie theater in Frederick, Maryland, accompanied by a caretaker to see the movie Zero Dark Thirty. Saylor had the genetic condition known as Down Syndrome, along with intellectual disabilities.

After the movie ended, he told his caretaker he wanted to see the movie again and began cursing when she refused. The caretaker called his mother who told her to wait him out and his attitude would change. The caretaker left Saylor in front of the theater to get the car hoping he would have settled down in the meantime. When she returned, Ethan had re-entered the theater and was being told by the manager he had to leave.

The caretaker told the manager she was having a little issue with Ethan, and she would handle it as they just needed to be patient. The theater manager called the mall security office who sent three off-duty deputy sheriffs who were moonlighting as security guards.

Ethan's caretaker explained to the officers that he had Down Syndrome and if they spoke to him, he would start cursing. One deputy threatened to arrest Ethan after he started cursing him. The caretaker further warned the deputies that if they grabbed or touched him, he would "freak out." Regardless, deputies grabbed Saylor, who weighed nearly 300 lbs., and wrestled him to the floor where he was handcuffed.

During the incident, Saylor began screaming "mommy, mommy, it hurts" as the deputies continued to wrestle him to the floor. This was corroborated by several witnesses.

Saylor began experiencing medical distress and died in the theater before his mother arrived. The death was due to a fractured larynx that led to asphyxiation, and the death was ruled a homicide by the medical examiner.

A civil lawsuit was filed against the deputies and the theater. The case was moved to federal court in an attempt to dismiss the case, but a federal judge ordered the case go to trial.

In April of 2018, the lawsuit was settled for nearly $2 million. After his death, the Ethan Saylor Alliance was formed by the Maryland Department of Disabilities in part to educate law enforcement officers on special needs of those with Developmental and Intellectual Disabilities.

Command Hallucinations / Schizophrenia Esteban Santiago, Fort Lauderdale Airport Shooting

In August of 2016, Santiago was working as an armed security guard in Anchorage, Alaska, when he informed family members that he was hearing voices and being chased.

In November, Santiago walked into the Anchorage Field Office of the FBI and reported he was being controlled by the government and that the CIA was trying to make him join ISIS. After determining he was not a terrorist threat, Santiago was turned over to the Anchorage Police Department who confiscated a handgun. The Police Chief stated Santiago was having terroristic thoughts, and that Santiago believed he was being instructed by ISIS.

Santiago was committed to a psychiatric facility but was released a couple days later. Since he was not adjudicated as mentally ill by the mental health facility his handgun was returned to him in December upon his request.

On January 5, 2017, Santiago bought a one-way plane ticket to Ft. Lauderdale, Florida. His only checked baggage was a handgun. On January 6, he arrived at Ft. Lauderdale / Hollywood International Airport and retrieved his handgun from baggage claims. He then entered a restroom where he loaded the weapon.

Santiago then exited the restroom and began shooting into the crowds, killing 5 people and injuring 6 more. He then laid on the floor as police officers converged on him and surrendered. He stated he was programmed to act.

According to family members, Santiago had begun experiencing mental illness after his return from Iraq while serving with the Puerto Rico National Guard. He later joined the Alaskan National Guard but was discharged because of performance issues.

After his arrest, Santiago was diagnosed with Schizophrenia. On May 23, 2018, Santiago pleaded guilty to 5 counts of murder to avoid the death penalty and was sentenced to 5 consecutive life sentences plus 120 years in prison.

Schizophrenia
Charleena Lyles and Seattle Police Department

On June 5, 2017, Seattle police officers responded to a call from Charleena Lyles regarding a domestic violence complaint against her boyfriend. When officers walked into the apartment, Ms. Lyles was holding a large pair of scissors while sitting next to her daughter on a couch in a threatening manner.

Ms. Lyles then stated "ain't none of you leaving here today." She then made statements the she could "morph into a wolf" and that she "could clone her daughter" along with other bizarre statements.

Police officers were eventually able to talk her into letting the child go and surrendering. She was arrested and was in jail for 12 days until a judge released her with the requirement that she seek psychological treatment, which she did not.

After her release on June 18, Ms. Lyles again called police to her home regarding a burglary. Two officers were dispatched because of the previous incident, including one of the officers responding who had been involved in the previous incident with Ms. Lyles.

As officers began repeating the list of items stolen, Ms. Lyles suddenly produced a large knife. Officers shot Ms. Lyles 7 times and she died at the scene. Neither officer was carrying a Taser as department policy required.

Bipolar Disorder
Rubin Herrera and LAPD

On December 29, 2015, LAPD officers responded to an apartment complex where Rubin Herrera had been throwing rocks against the building and assaulting residents. Herrera lived nearby and had been diagnosed with Bipolar Disorder. He had stopped taking his prescribed medications.

After a physical altercation with Herrera in which he had tried to grab one of the officer's weapon, he was subdued and taken to the hospital where he and officers were treated for injuries. Herrera was handcuffed to the bed while being treated.

Once Herrera was cleared for release by medical personnel, two different officers arrived to transport him to jail. When the handcuffs were removed, Herrera picked up a metal stool and began swinging it at officers who used a Taser with no effect. Herrera then grabbed an officer's weapon again in an attempt to remove it from the holster.

The officer was able to retain his weapon and fired one shot killing Herrera. LAPD was cleared of any wrongdoing.

Delusional Disorder
Margaret Mary "Peggy" Ray Stalking Case

Peggy Ray suffered from Erotomania Delusional Disorder where the person believes that someone, usually someone famous or prominent, is in love with them. Ms. Ray was the renown stalker of television host David Letterman and astronaut Story Musgrave.

Ms. Ray was first arrested after failing to pay a toll at the Lincoln Tunnels while driving Letterman's Porsche which she had stolen. She identified herself as Letterman's wife and her four-year old son as Letterman's child. She was arrested several times over a period of years for trespassing and had several restraining orders filed against her. Ray spent a total of 20 months in jail and 14 months in psychiatric care during her obsession with Mr. Letterman.

Each time she was committed and given medication she would improve. However, after being released each time, she would stop taking medication, and her mental condition would deteriorate again. She was homeless from time to time, and wandered around the country.

After David Letterman, Ms. Ray began stalking astronaut Story Musgrave. Since delusional disorders do not necessarily impede functioning like with schizophrenia, she was able to pose as a reporter and interviewed Musgrave in Houston before she started trespassing on his property in Florida. Ms. Ray repeated another series of incarcerations in jail and commitments to mental health facilities as before. After serving time in jail for the last time, Ray was committed to psychiatric care. She was finally released in 1998 after her illness was deemed to have improved.

After her release in Florida, Ms. Ray moved to Colorado. On October 5, 1998, she knelt down in front of a speeding train and committed suicide.

Oppositional Defiant Disorder
Deputy Ben Fields

On October 28, 2015, Deputy Ben Fields was working as a School Resource Officer in Richland County, NC, when he was called to a classroom regarding a disruptive and noncompliant student.

A 16-year-old female student had refused to relinquish her cell phone to school administrators in violation of school policies. She had been asked to leave the classroom and refused. Deputy Fields asked her to stand and again she refused this directive. In what the deputy claimed was an attempt to separate her from her desk, Fields slammed her desk backwards and dragged her across the floor.

According to all accounts, the student was disruptive, argumentative, and noncompliant with rules. School officials and students reported that the female had a lengthy history of disruptive behavior. Many of the students who witnessed the incident reported that the student was the instigator.

Regardless, Fields was fired for not using tactical communications to get her to comply and for the excessive use of force. The Department of Justice declined to bring charges against the deputy.

Posttraumatic Stress Disorder
Suicide by Cop – Nikkolas Lookabill

Nikkolas Lookabill served a tour of duty in Iraq and returned to his home town of Vancouver, Washington, in May 2010 after being diagnosed with PTSD.

On September 7, 2010, Lookabill got into an argument with his girlfriend at her apartment. She asked him to leave because she was becoming fearful of his erratic behavior. Lookabill left the apartment after becoming intoxicated and was in possession of a .45 caliber handgun. He was also taking anti-depressant medications that evening for depression.

Nearby residents called the Vancouver police department after observing Lookabill staggering along the street. He had also brandished the weapon at a couple of people asking them if they were a "friend or enemy." Lookabill continued to walk to a neighborhood convenience store where he purchased and began drinking cans of caffeinated alcohol beverages.

After leaving the store, Lookabill was confronted by police officers. He produced the handgun and was asked to drop the weapon. He slowly walked backwards and assumed a crouched position, taunting the officers. He then stood up and placed the gun in the pocket of a hooded sweatshirt and said "come and get it."

During negotiations with Lookabill, he stated that he had wanted to join the police force after his military service but knew that wasn't possible now. He then told officers to shoot him. Officers repeatedly told him not to make a move toward the gun. After being told this, he repeatedly taunted officers by moving his hands toward the pocket and saying "like this" in response to their warnings.

Finally, he reached toward his pocket as if to retrieve the gun and was shot 13 times.

Lookabill died at the scene.

Intermittent Explosive Disorder
Eric Smith

14-year-old Eric Smith made national news after being found guilty of murder. Smith, who was 13 years old at the time of the murder looked much younger than his stated age. He had lured a 4-year-old boy into the woods near Bath, New York, and crushed his head with a rock.

Smith later confessed to the murder stating he led 4-year-old Derrick Robie on what he told the boy was supposed to be a shortcut on the way home from a day camp. Eric choked the young boy and then crushed his head with a 26-pound rock. He then sodomized the body with a stick.

Smith was diagnosed with intermittent explosive disorder which is characterized by uncontrollable violent impulses. No motive was given for the attack although this disorder usually involves aggression for which there is no reasoning or very little provocation.

However, Eric was tried as an adult and the diagnosis was unsuccessful as a defense.

Eric Smith sat emotionless when he was sentenced to 9 years to life in prison.

Substance Induced Disorders
Alton Sterling and Baton Rouge Police

On July 5, 2016, Baton Rouge police were called to a convenience store regarding a man who had threatened someone with a gun. Police encountered Alton Sterling who refused to comply with orders to put his hands on the car to be searched for the reported weapon.

One officer then slammed Sterling onto the car and pulled his weapon from his holster and pointed it at Sterling's head yelling "I'll shoot you in the fucking head" along with several other profanity laced statements. These tactics had no effect. The officer then ordered another officer to use a taser on Sterling, which also had no effect. Sterling was then tackled to the ground where he continued to resist arrest.

At this point, according to the officer's statements, it appeared Sterling was trying to get the gun from his pocket. Officers shot him 6 times, and he died at the scene. An autopsy revealed that Sterling had cocaine, alcohol, methamphetamines, hydrocodone, and marijuana in his blood.

No criminal charges were brought against the officers. However, the officer who pulled his weapon and pointed it at Sterling's head while screaming profanities was fired for violating policies, including failing to contain his temper. Lawsuits were filed against the officer.

Lawsuits are pending.

Suicide by Cop
Micah Jester and Austin Police

On October 16, 2016, the husband of Micah Jester called the Austin, Texas

Police Department and reported his wife was behaving erratically. He also stated that she was armed with a handgun.

When officers arrived, Micah confronted them on the sidewalk outside her home with the handgun and began shouting "shoot me, shoot me, kill me." After being told to drop the weapon she continued walking toward the officers, they shot her.

While she was lying on the ground and still alive, the gun was underneath her and still in her hand. Officers commanded her to produce and surrender the handgun. She again refused to produce or surrender the gun and repeated saying "kill me." Officers shot Jester again, and she died at the scene.

The weapon turned out to be a BB gun.

Ten years earlier, Jester's father had been shot and killed by police officers in Florida after he pointed a toy pistol at them during a traffic stop. According to a relative, the shooting of her father had a profound effect on Jester, who was 16 years old when he died.

Autism

Eric Parsa and Jefferson Parish Sheriff's Office

Eric Parsa was a 16-year-old boy with severe autism. On January 19, 2020, he became upset outside a mall and began slapping himself in the head while with his parents. As his father intervened, Eric began slapping and biting the man causing him to bleed. Eric's mother asked a bystander to call the police for assistance since her son was obese and difficult to manage physically.

A deputy who provided security at the mall arrived and initially restrained the youth after he was slapped and bitten as well. The deputy wrestled Eric to the ground, placed him in handcuffs, and then sat on his back until another deputy arrived. The second deputy then say on Eric's back to relieve the first one. Eric was allegedly in prone position with someone sitting on him for over 9 minutes before going limp. He died while being transported in an ambulance on the way to the hospital.

The cause of death was listed as excited delirium and the prone position due to his obesity. Lawsuits are pending.

Autism

Linden Cameron and Salt Lake City Police

In September, 2020, the mother of 13-year-old Linden Cameron called the Salt Lake City Police Department for assistance with her son who has Asperger's Syndrome. He had become upset over a family issue and appeared to have a 'mental breakdown' in the words of his mother. There was a report that he may have been armed, but no gun was ever observed or found. The youth was in the house when officers arrived.

As police arrived, Linden ran from the house and one officer began chasing him. Shortly after, the officer shot Linden 11 times causing multiple wounds which he survived.

In November, 2020, a lawsuit was filed on behalf of the family alleging use of force contrary to police policy, and lack of training on how to handle the mentally ill among other reasons.

Posttraumatic Stress Disorder

Nitro, WV, Police Department

In February, 2020, Nitro, West Virginia police officers answered a call of someone shooting a rifle at a local business. Officers soon located a man carrying an AK-47 assault rifle in the neighborhood.

The 30-year-old man was identified as a local veteran who was known to suffer from PTSD and was delusional. The man reported that he was shooting at people and giant rats that were following him and that they disintegrated when he shot them.

The man had also shot several rounds inside his apartment and at his porch as he was fleeing the home.

No one was injured and he was charged with wanton endangerment.

Suicidal Behavior

Dustin Pigeon and Oklahoma City Police

On November 15, 2017, Dustin Pigeon called 911 and stated he was going to commit suicide.

When the first officers arrived, they found Pigeon standing in his yard with a can of lighter fluid and a cigarette lighter in his hands. As the officers tried to negotiate with him, a supervisor arrived on the scene. The sergeant exited his vehicle about the same time Pigeon began squirting fluid on his head and body.

The initial officers correctly discharged a non-lethal bean bag round from a shotgun to stun and distract the suicidal man.

Sgt. Sweeney immediately shot Pigeon several times with his firearm, killing the unarmed man.

Sweeney was found guilty of murder and sentenced to prison.

Excited Delirium

Adam Trammell – West Milwaukee Police Department

On May 25, 2017, police were called to an apartment building regarding a mentally ill man standing naked in the hallway. Upon arriving, they were told by residents that the man had gone back into his apartment and now appeared to be flooding the floor.

Officers failed to get a response by knocking on the door and finally forced the door open to conduct a welfare check. They repeatedly called the name Brandon as they entered, even though the subjects name was Adam.

They found Adam naked in the shower. They repeatedly ordered him to get out but Adam refused and splashed water on one of the officers. Adam was warned if he didn't get out of the shower, they would have to user a taser.

The officer then tased the subject between 15 and 18 times within a few minutes while naked and wet inside the shower. Trammell began resisting officers while being tased and collapsed in the tub where he was handcuffed and subdued.

After removing him from the shower, paramedics inject Trammel with Ketamine. His breathing slowed and he then died.

The cause of death was ruled as excited delirium. One hour after his death, Trammell's body temperature was still an extraordinary 104 degrees.

The department settled a lawsuit for $2.5 million. The officers were not charged.

Excited Delirium

Elijah McClain – Aurora Colorado

On August 24, 2019, 23-year-old Elijah McClain was walking home from the store when an area resident called police to investigate his as a suspicious person because he was wearing a hood on his head.

When officer confronted McClain, he told them he was an introvert and often wore a 23-year-old hooded shirt. After questioning the man, officers claim they felt threatened and decided to restrain McClain. One officer used a chokehold as McClain struggled. He was finally handcuffed.

Moments later, paramedics from the Aurora fire department arrived and injected McClain with Ketamine.

He died 7 minutes later.

The paramedics were initial charged criminally and the family settled a federal civil rights claim against 3 officers and the 2 paramedics.

Excited Delirium

Daniel Prude – Rochester NY Police Department

On March 23, 2020, police received a call from the brother of Daniel Prude. The brother explained that Daniel had spent the night before in a mental health facility and upon release, he ingested PCP.

Prude had left his brother's home completely naked and was walking through the streets of Rochester.

When officers approached Prude, they ordered him to put his hands behind his back. He cooperated and was handcuffed and placed on the pavement. At this point Prude became highly agitated and began spitting on officers who deployed a mesh spit hood.

As Prude continued to try and stand, officers held him to the ground and used what the termed a "hypoglossal nerve technique" which involves jamming fingers into a nerve under the jaw as a method to gain compliance.

Prude stopped moving and speaking as officers continued to hold his head to the pavement until an officer noticed he was no longer breathing. He was taken to a hospital where he was declared brain dead and taken off life support.

The cause of death was determined to be asphyxia from restraint, excited delirium, and PCP intoxication. The manner of death was ruled a homicide.

Lawsuits are pending.

MI Report Writing

Phrases and Terms to Avoid in Report Writing

Written reports reflect the actions and decision making of officers answering calls for service and serve as a record of the officer's behavior, as well. In cases where physically force or deadly force occur, it is especially important that the narrative is absent of any biases, preconceived beliefs, or misconceptions about mental illness.

It is also important that the report or record of an incident details any and all efforts to de-escalate force and steps taken to minimize injuries to the person in keeping with recent court rulings that the use of force weighs heavily in the favor of someone with a mental disorder, particularly those who are not armed.

▶ United States Public Law 111-256, known as Rosa's Law, replaces the terms mental retardation and mental impairment with Intellectual Disability or Intellectual Development Disorder.

▶ On October 5, 2010, President Obama signed legislation requiring the federal government to replace the term "mental retardation" with "intellectual disability" in many areas of government. The measure known as Rosa's Law, will strip the terms "mental retardation" and" mentally retarded" from federal health, education and labor policy. "Intellectual disability' or "individual with an intellectual disability" will be inserted in their places.

Terms or phrases to avoid include:

Moron

Imbecile

Idiot

Feeble minded

Crazy or crazed

Lunatic

Insane

Mental

Schizo

Deranged

Nut job

Possessed

Retard or Tard

Psycho

Obviously, any police report should be absent of derogatory or condescending names, terms, or phrases. The reporting of incidents involving mentally ill or special needs individuals are highly sensitive with families and advocates of those with special needs.

APPENDIX

Medications Commonly Used to Treat Mental Illness and Likely to be Present on Calls for Service

Antipsychotic Drugs

Generic & Tradename

Chlorpromazine   (Thorazine)
Thioridazine   (Mellaril)
Fluphenazine   (Prolixin)
Fluphenazine   (Prolixin D)
Perphenazine   (Trilafon)
Trifluoperazine   (Stelazine)
Haloperidol   (Haldol)
Thiothixine   (Navane)
Loxapine   (Loxitane)
Molidone   (Moban)
Clozapine   (Clozaril)
Risperidone   (Risperdal)
Aripiprazole (Abilify)
Aripiprazole L   (Aristada)

Asenapine	(Saphris)
Iloperidone	(Fanapt)
Larasidone HCl	(Latuda)
Olanzapine	(Zyprexa)
Paliperidone	(Invega)
Quetiapine	(Seroquel)
Ziprasidone	(Geodon)

Antidepressants

Generic & Tradename

Tranylcypromine (Parnate)	Sertraline (Zoloft)
Phenelzine (Nardil)	Paroxetine (Paxil)
Fluoxetine (Prozac)	Bupropion (Wellbutrin)
Trazodone (Desyrel)	Venlafaxine (Effexor)
Citalopram	(Celexa)
Amitriptyline	(Elavil)

Imipramine	(Tofranil)
Desipramine	(Norpramin)
Nortriptyline	(Pamelor)
Protriptyline	(Vivactil)
Doxepin	(Sinequan)
Maprotiline	(Ludiomil)
Amoxapine	(Asendin)
Clomipramine	(Anafril)

Antianxiety Drugs

Generic & Tradename

Diazepam	(Valium)
Chlordiazepoxide	(Librium)
Clorazepate	(Tranxene)
Prazepam	(Centrax)
Halazepam	(Paxipam)
Lorazepam	(Ativan)
Alprazolam	(Xanax)
Oxazepam	(Serax)
Clonazepam	(Klonipin)
Buspirone	(Buspar)
Hydroxyzine	(Atarax) (Vistaril)

Bipolar Disorder Medications

Generic & Tradename

Aripiprazole (Abilify)
Asenapine   (Saphris)
Cariprazine   (Vraylar)
Clozapine   (Clozaril)
Lurasidone HCl   (Latuda)
Olanzapine   (Zyprexa)
Quetiapine   (Seroquel)
Risperidone   (Risperdol)
Ziprasidone   (Geodon)

Generic and Trade Names of Psychotropic Drugs

Abilify – trade name for the antipsychotic medication Aripiprazole.

Alprazolam - generic name for the antianxiety medication Xanax

Amitriptyline - generic name for the antidepressant Elavil.

Amoxapine - generic name for the antidepressant Asendin.

Anafranil - trade name for the generic antidepressant Clomipramine.

Aripiprazole – generic name for antipsychotic medication Abilify.

Aripiprazole L – generic name for antipsychotic medication Aristada.

Aristada – trade name for antipsychotic medication Aripiprazole L.

Asenapine – generic name for antipsychotic medication Saphris.

Asendin - trade name for the antidepressant Amoxipine.

Atarax – trade name for antianxiety medication Hydroxyzine.

Ativan - trade name for the antianxiety medication Lorazepam.

Buproprion - generic name for the antidepressant Wellbutrin.

Buspar - trade name for the antianxiety medication Buspirone.

Buspirone - generic name for the antianxiety medication Buspar.

Cariprazine – generic name for bipolar medication Vraylar.

Chlordiazepoxide - generic name for the antianxiety medication Librium.

Chlorazepate - generic name for the antianxiety medication Traxene.

Chloropromazine - generic for the antipsychotic medication Thorazine.

Centrax - trade name for the antianxiety medication Prazepam.

Citalopram – generic for antidepressant Celexa.

Clomipramine - generic name for the antidepressant Anafranil.

Clonazepam - generic for the antidepressant Klonipin.

Clozapine - generic name for the antipsychotic medication Clozaril.

Clozaril - trade name for the antipsychotic medication Clozapine.

Cylert - medication used in the treatment of Attention-Deficit Hyperactivity Disorder (ADHA).

Depakote - trade name for the antimanic medication Valporic Acid.

Desipramine - generic name for the antidepressant Norpramin.

Desyrel - trade name for the antidepressant Trazodone.

Diazepam - generic name for the antianxiety medication Valium.

Doxepine - generic name for the antidepressant Sinequan.

Effexor - trade name for the antidepressant Venlafaxine.

Elavil - trade name for the antidepressant Amitriptyline.

Fanapt – trade name for antipsychotic medication Iloperidone

Fluphenazine - generic name for the antipsychotic medication Prolixin.

Fluoxetine - generic name for the antidepressant Prozac.

Geodon – trade name for antipsychotic medication Ziprasidone.

Halazepam - generic name for the antianxiety medication Paxipam.

Haldol - trade name for the antipsychotic medication Haloperidol.

Haloperidol - generic name for the antipsychotic medication Haldol, an anti-schizophrenic drug found in the butyrophenones class of chemicals.

Hydroxyzine – generic for antianxiety medication Atarax or Vistaril.

Iloperidone – generic name for antipsychotic medication Fanapt.

Imipramine - generic name for the antidepressant Tofranil.

Klonipin - trade name for the antianxiety medication Clonazepam.

Lurasidone HCl – generic name for antipsychotic medication Latuda.

Latuda – trade name for antipsychotic medication Lurasidone HCl.

Librium - trade name for the antianxiety medication Chlodiazepoxide.

Lithium - a metallic ion used as an antimanic medication in the treatment of Bipolar Disorder.

Invega – trade name for antipsychotic medication Paliperidone.

Lorazepam - generic name of the antianxiety medication Ativan.

Loxapine - generic name of the antipsychotic medication Loxitane.

Loxitane - trade name of the antipsychotic medication Loxapine.

Ludiomil - trade name of the antidepressant Maprotiline.

Maprotiline - generic name of the antidepressant Ludiomil.

Mellaril - trade name of the antipsychotic medication Thioridazine.

Moban - trade name of the antipsychotic medication Molindone.

Molindone - generic name of the antipsychotic medication Moban.

Nardil - trade name of the antidepressant Phenelzime.

Navane - trade name of the antipsychotic medication Thiothixine.

Norpramin - trade name of the antidepressant Desipramine.

Nortriptyline - generic name of the antidepressant Pamelor.

Olanzapine – generic name for antipsychotic medication Zyprexa

Oxazepam - generic name of the antianxiety medication Serax.

Paliperidone – generic for antipsychotic medication Invega

Pamelor - trade name for the antidepressant Nortriptyline.

Parnate - trade name for the antidepressant Tranylcypromine.

Paroxetine - generic name for the antidepressant Paxil.

Paxil - trade name for the antidepressant Paroxetine.

Paxipam - trade name for the antianxiety medication Halazepam.

Perphenazine - generic name for the antipsychotic medication Trilafon.

Phenelzine - generic name for the antidepressant Nardil.

Prazepam - generic name for the antianxiety medication Centrax.

Prolixin - trade name for the antipsychotic medication Fluphenazine.

Protriptyline - generic name for the antidepressant Vivactil.

Prozac - popular trade name of the antidepressant Fluoxetine.

Quetiapine – generic name for antipsychotic medication Seroquel.

Risperdal - trade name of the antipsychotic medication Risperidone.

Risperidone - generic name of the antipsychotic medication Risperdal.

Ritalin - popular trade name for methylphenidate used in the treatment of Attention-Deficit Hyperactivity Disorder (ADHA).

Serax - trade name of the antianxiety medication Oxazepam.

Seroquel – trade name for antipsychotic medication Quetiapine.

Sertaline - generic name of the antidepressant Zoloft.

Sinequan - trade name of the antidepressant Doxepine.

Stelazine - trade name of the antipsychotic medication Trifluoperazine.

Thiothixine - generic name for the antipsychotic medication Navane.

Thioridazine - generic name for the antipsychotic medication Mellaril.

Thorazine - trade name for the antipsychotic medication Chlorpromazine.

Tofranil - trade name for the antidepressant medication Imipramine.

Tranylcypromine - generic name for the antidepressant Parnate.

Traxene - trade name for the antianxiety medication Chlorazepate.

Trazodone - generic name for the antidepressant Desyrel.

Tricyclic antidepressants - a class of antidepressant medications that include Imipramine.

Trifluoperazine - generic name for the antipsychotic medication Stelazine.

Valium - trade name for the antianxiety medication Diazepam.

Valporic Acid - generic name for the anti-manic medication Depakote.

Venlafaxine - generic name for the antidepressant Effexor.

Vistaril – trade name for antianxiety medication Hydroxydine.

Vivactil - trade name of the antidepressant medication Protriptyline.

Vraylar – trade name for bipolar medication Cariprazine.

Wellbutrin - trade name of the antidepressant Bupropion.

Xanax - trade name of the antianxiety medication Alprazolam.

Zoloft - trade name of the antidepressant medication Sertaline.

Ziprasidone – generic for bipolar medication Geodon.

Zyprexa trade name for antipsychotic medication Olanzapine.

The presence of these medications should only direct police and other law enforcement personnel to inquire further with a trained physician or mental health professionals as to the significance of the medication.

Definitions of Associated Terms

Alcohol Intoxication and Withdrawal are the most common types of Alcohol Induced Disorders.

Alzheimer's Disease is the most common form of Dementia listed under Neurocognitive Disorders.

Amnesia is the sudden inability to recall important personal information.

Antisocial Personality Disorder is most associated with criminality but is only one of several personality disorders.

Anxiety Disorders are disorders that involve fear, panic, and anxiousness such as Panic Attacks, Panic Disorder, Agoraphobia (fear of open spaces) to mention a few.

Autism is one of several Neurodevelopmental Disorders which affect the ability to communicate in social and other settings and have patterns of behavior that are repetitive and inflexible.

Bipolar Disorder was previously known as Manic – Depression and involves episodes of mania and depression, and in severe cases delusional thinking.

Borderline Personality Disorder involves a pattern of unstable and stormy relationships, difficulty in managing anger, leading to risky and self-damaging behavior including suicidal thoughts and actions.

Brief Psychotic Disorder has the same features as Schizophrenia Spectrum Disorders but is less severe and shorter in duration.

Cannabis Intoxication and Withdrawal are another common type of Substance Induced Disorders.

Conduct Disorder is behavior usually in adolescent years in which major age-appropriate rules are broken, e.g., drinking, and criminal behavior is evident.

Delirium is an occurrence of disorientation, memory problems, lack of awareness and attention often associated with prolonged use of alcohol or other substances.

Delusions are firm and false beliefs in spite of all evidence to the contrary. Delusions may be about things that could occur, e.g., being followed by the CIA, or bizarre beliefs about things that are not possible, like being abducted by aliens. Others are erotomania, jealousy, persecutory, grandiose and somatic to name a few.

Depression is a common disorder in which sadness may be out of proportion to the circumstances.

Dissociative Identity Disorder was formerly known as Multiple Personalities, a rare occurrence in which there exists two separate ego states.

Hallucinations are different from delusions as they are experiences involving hearing, sight, vision, taste, touch, and bodily sensations.

Histrionic Personality Disorder involves an excessive display emotions and attention seeking and abrupt mood changes that may present themselves in gestures of suicidal behavior.

Intellectual Disabilities occur during development and affect intellectual and social functioning that may be mild, moderate, severe, or profound, each level requiring higher levels of supervision.

Intermittent Explosive Disorder is an impulse control disorder in which one cannot control violent impulses and temper.

Kleptomania is the impulsive urge to steal items, usually inexpensive, which are not needed or used for economic or other gain, and in many cases the person could easily afford to purchase.

Mood Disorders commonly refers to disorders such as Major Depression and Dysthymia (depressed mood) and other disorders affecting one's mood.

Obsessive-Compulsive Personality Disorder involves a rigid and inflexible preoccupation with order, perfection, rules and regulations, affecting personal relationships and occupational performance.

Opioid Intoxication is another Substance Induced Disorder by the use of opioids.

Opposition Defiant Disorder usually presents itself in children before age thirteen and involves defiance of adult requests, argumentative behavior, and disruptive behavior.

Panic Attacks are sudden occurrences in which the person feels overwhelmed with fear causing physiological discomforts.

Paranoid Personality Disorder involves beliefs that people are somehow plotting or deceiving them in spite of evidence to the contrary, or with a lack of evidence may believe their spouse or significant other is cheating on them. They are more litigious and more often file complaints against neighbors or others.

Paraphilias are a group of abnormal sexual behaviors involving non-human objects, children and other non-consenting persons, or the humiliation or suffering of one's self or partner.

Personality Disorders are a group of behaviors involving how someone perceives themselves, others, or events and how they respond to them leading to personal relationship issues and in some cases self-damaging behavior. Paranoid, Narcissistic, Borderline, Histrionic, and Dependent Personalities are a few examples.

Posttraumatic Stress Disorder is a response to an event in which the person experiences or witness's death, serious injury, or sexual assault or over exposure to these distressing events.

Pyromania is an impulsive control disorder involving urges to set fires as a release of built-up tensions with an inordinate interest in watching fires and fire paraphernalia. Fire setting is not done for profit, revenge, or other purpose.

Schizoid Personality Disorder involves patterns of estrangement and detachment from family and friends, "loners" who lack desire for interpersonal relationships, who prefer living isolated from others, sometimes found in the homeless population.

Schizophrenia is a disorder involving hallucinations, delusions, disorganized behavior, motor skills, or disorganized language or communications skills.

Schizotypal Personality Disorder involves detachment and estrangement found in Schizoid Personality Disorder but involves more bizarre and odd outward behaviors, sometimes found in the homeless population.

Stalking is not a mental disorder of itself but in a large number of cases they have been diagnosed with disorders such as Borderline Personality Disorder, Histrionic Personality Disorder and Delusional Disorders.

Suicide by Cop is a phenomenon where persons wanting to die create a situation where responding police officers are forced to use deadly force against them.

References

American Psychiatric Association: Diagnostic and Statistical Manual of Mental Disorders, Fifth Edition. Arlington, VA, 2013

The Clinicians Handbook: Integrated Diagnostics, Assessment, and Intervention in Adult and Adolescent Psychopathy, Fourth Edition. Robert G. Meyer, Sarah E. Deitsch 1996.

Forensic Psychology: A Guide for Criminal Justice Professionals, Robert D. Newell, West Virginia University of Parkersburg.

National Alliance on Mental Illness. (NAMI)

National Institute on Mental Health. (NIH)

Substance Abuse and Mental Health Services Administration. (SAMHSA)

Research of Mental Hygiene Laws and Statutes in the Unites States.

Treatment Advocacy Center, State Standards for Assisted Treatment, Civil Commitment Criteria for Inpatient or Outpatient Psychiatric Treatment, 2011.

Armstrong v. Town of Pinehurst, U.S. Supreme Court of Appeals, 4th Circuit, No. 15-1191

Tarasoff v. University of California Regents, 17 Cal. 3d 425 (1976)

R.D. Newell & Associates, LLC

bobnewell1@outlook.com

Parkersburg, WV

Notes

Notes

Notes

Notes